The Art of South Florida Gardening

A unique guide to planning, planting,
and making your subtropical
garden grow

by Harold Songdahl
and Coralee Leon

Illustrations by George Curtis

Plant drawings by Coralee Leon

 Pineapple Press, Inc.
Sarasota, Florida

Inquiries should be addressed to:
Pineapple Press, Inc.
P. O. Box 3899
Sarasota, FL 34230

LIBRARY OF CONGRESS
CATALOGING IN PUBLICATION DATA

Songdahl, Harold.
    The art of south Florida gardening : a unique guide to
planning, planting, and making your sub-tropical garden grow
/by Harold Songdahl and Coralee Leon : illustrations by George
Curtis. -- 1st ed.
                p.   cm.
        Includes index.
        ISBN 1-56164-088-3 (pbk. : alk. paper)
        1. Landscape gardening--Florida.   I. Leon, Coralee.   II. Title.
SB473.S595 1995
635.9'09759--dc20   95-42720
                                                                      CIP

First Edition
10 9 8 7 6 5 4 3 2

Design by Coralee Leon
Printed and bound by Quebecor/Fairfield, Fairfield, Pennsylvania

The authors wish to acknowledge
the kindness of those who helped.

For their invaluable expert contributions
to the text, Dr. Monroe Birdsey, South Florida
horticulturist and esteemed university
professor; Seymour Goldwebber, University of
Florida extension agent emeritus;
Ray Glenn, long-time Florida nurseryman;
Dee Hull, Dade County Agricultural Agent;
Robert J. Knight, Jr., former research
horticulturist, USDA, now with the University
of Florida at Homestead; and Mary Schneider,
head of the Master Gardeners program
in Dade County.

For production assistance with Mr. Curtis's
delightful drawings, Kathy Romero
of Matrix 2, Miami.

For offering exceedingly helpful input from
the readers' point of view, South Florida
friends and gardeners Laura Daigle,
Virginia M. Schrenker, and June Sutton; and
Darryl the wonderful, witty, wise,
and exceedingly handsome.

And for always letting us back into the house
when we're grubby, sweaty, and smelling of
fertilizer, this book is dedicated with love

to Millie and Michael

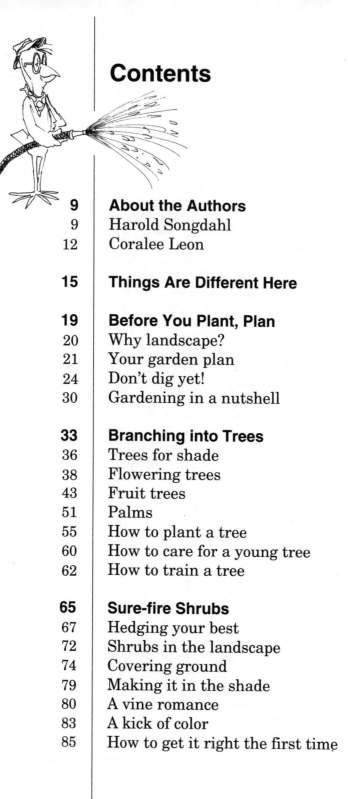

Contents

About the Authors

arold Songdahl

Harold Songdahl was born in Miami on April Fool's Day, 1931. He was educated in botany, but his intimate knowledge of horticulture and gardening comes from a lifetime of growing and living with plants. To Harold, plants are fascinating and fun. They always have been.

By the age of six, Harold was digging up interesting seedlings from vacant lots and bringing them home to show his mother. By nine, he had begun to experiment with harvesting seeds. Among his favorites were those of the Bright Eyes periwinkles—white with red centers, then already fairly rare—which he planted in the yard. He also grew a cherry hedge from seed to a height of 12 inches before yanking it out, having learned another early lesson: Cherry hedges need a lot of trimming.

Harold's enthusiasm was encouraged by his father, a master mariner who loved working with plants during his relatively brief periods ashore. It was from his dad that Harold learned how to propagate plants by air layering their branches and by grafting and budding. He remembers his father creating wondrous trees that produced fruit salads of oranges, grapefruit, and limes, and hibiscus bushes that bloomed in many colors.

But Harold was anything but a horti-nerd. He played left tackle on the unde-feated 1949 Miami Senior High foot-ball team. He and his buddies kayaked and sailed together on Biscayne Bay, spearfished using homemade Hawai-ian slings, and, before there was a Rick-enbacker Causeway, swam across to Virginia Key. There were frequent ad-ventures into the Everglades—which was a bit easier then because, in Mi-ami at least, the end of the civilized world was Le Jeune Road.

He explored South Florida from sea to shining gulf, from Lake Okeechobee to Florida Bay, learning its topography and flora at first hand: Everglades marshes, pinelands, ham-mocks, pinnacle rock, sand, and the rocky bluffs from the ice ages, which scientists still come to study where they erupt in Coconut Grove at the edges of manicured lawns along South Bayshore Drive.

Thousands of orchids, ferns, and bromeli-ads were to be found in the wild in those days, and each hardwood hammock was home to its own unique variety, distinctively marked, of tree snail. Many of the old hammocks are now gone, their hundreds of live oaks and the spe-cies they sheltered replaced by houses and roads and invidious melaleuca trees.

By the time he graduated from the Uni-versity of Miami, Harold had served four years in the United States Navy. During the Korean War he'd been posted at the naval air station in Hawaii, where he discovered plant life very much like that of South Florida, though much more lush owing to the rich volcanic soils.

Back home at his first job, with the sheriff's

office, he would startle his patrol partners by suddenly screeching to a halt to get a better look at, and sometimes collect, an unusual plant he'd spotted along the road. Inevitably his natural interests and background led him to professional horticulture, and he has never left it.

During his career in the South Florida foliage, nursery, and landscaping industries, Harold has earned his reputation as one of the most knowledgeable horticulturists in the region. He has lived, worked, and gardened on every kind of South Florida soil, and has personally grown at least one of just about every kind of plant that will grow here, as well as some that aren't supposed to.

He has introduced to South Florida, and propagated for commercial distribution, several popular landscape plants, including the fountainlike fakahatchee grass, the ground cover Blue Daze, and the purslane varieties Fireglow, Goldenglow, and Passionglow. Harold is also a successful private gardening consultant, making personal "garden calls" to businesses, institutions, condominiums, and family homes throughout South Florida, and serving as a special emissary for the Dade County Cooperative Extension Service.

Blue Daze

A longtime member of the Florida Nurserymen and Growers Association (FNGA), Harold has served as secretary and president of the Dade County Chapter, and he turned the small internal Dade County Nursery Report into a respected industry-wide publication. But he is perhaps most widely known as the Tropical Plant Man, a wise and witty radio personality whose call-in gardening programs, heard all around South Florida and the Bahamas, made him famous for his solid information, rich store of Miami lore, and down-home sense of humor. He is a sought-after speaker for gatherings of commercial growers as well as amateur gardeners.

Harold lives in South Dade with his wife, Millie, and their ever-changing garden. Their children, Bruce, Lynn, and Karen, live nearby with their families and many pets.

Coralee Leon

Writer Coralee Leon became acquainted with Harold through his radio program. Like many of his loyal listeners, she was an enthusiastic gardener transplanted from up north, struggling to make the adjustment from one growing season to four, and alien to the idiosyncrasies of subtropical plants and the astonishingly unyielding rocky South Dade soil.

Under Harold's entertaining broadcast guidance, Coralee was able to transform a mystery tree in her yard that had borne tough rubbery nutlike objects one year into one that produced sweet, juicy tangerines the next. In fact she attributes most of her South Florida gardening successes to advice gleaned from her radio mentor on Saturday mornings over the airwaves. She approached him with the idea of doing a project together. The partnership, they decided, would be an ideal combination of his gardening expertise and her gardening enthusiasm and writing talents.

Educated at New York University, Coralee Leon began her career with newspapers in New York and New Jersey, then went on to *House & Garden* magazine, first as a writer, later as managing editor. Her articles and short stories have appeared in *Redbook, Glamour, Vogue, The Ladies' Home Journal, Self, House Beautiful*, and *The New York Times*.

She ghost-wrote *Billy Baldwin Decorates* and *Billy Baldwin Remembers* with the late New York decorator, Billy Baldwin, and *More Needlepoint Design* with Palm Beach needlepoint artist and designer Louis J. Gartner. *Psychic Summer*, a thriller she wrote in collaboration with her friend Arnold Copper, sold more than 350,000 copies in paperback.

Coralee and her husband, Michael Philpot, live in South Dade County with their golden retriever, Willie. Her son Darryl, a U.S. Air Force officer, and his wife Keri, are graduates of Florida State University.

Things Are
Different Here

t's something long-term South Floridians know and newcomers learn fast: South Florida gardening is unique.

Take a look at the "zone map" of any good national garden catalog: It will be full of gorgeous, tempting plants, nearly all of which will thrive in zones 3 through 9. South Florida occupies zone 10.

Nowhere else in the continental United States, with the exception of a few isolated spots in southern California and Texas, are temperatures as warm in winter as they are here. The finger of Florida, dipped into the warm waters of the Atlantic's Gulfstream and the Gulf of Mexico, is not just heated, but humidified, as far north as Lake Okeechobee, and on up the coastlines as far as Tampa Bay on the west and Cape Canaveral on the east.

South Florida is subtropical. And subtropical gardens live by different rules.

Subtropical plants can be temperamental, thriving in relatively small ranges of habitat and stubbornly refusing to grow anywhere else. Some that thrive in Key West won't grow in Tampa. Some, in fact, can't make it north of Miami's Flagler Street. Most northern plants, much as we wish, hard as we try, don't stand much of a chance here. But then again, neither do penguins or timber wolves. And if our gardens are too hot for tulips and foreign to forsythia, they are paradise for poinsettias, orchids, hibiscus, bougainvilleas, and poinciana trees—in short, some of the most spectacular plants, flowers, and trees in the world.

Plants in South Florida have a rather long growing season: 24 hours a day, seven days a week, 52 weeks a year. No matter what the time of year, there are always flowers in bloom. We don't have exceedingly tall trees, but there are lots of them. The curbside vegetative trash pile full of fronds, branches, and hedge clippings is, in many communities, a South Florida tradition.

Rain plays a precipitous part in South Florida gardens, gushing down in summer (assuring convocations of insects and fungus as well as powerful vegetative growth), and withholding itself in winter, turning conscientious gardeners into conservationists.

Given the prodigious plant life in South Florida, it comes as a surprise to many that the soils here are just plain terrible. Northerners accustomed to the rich knee-deep loams of New Jersey and Michigan are aghast when they hear their spades clank against limestone rock three inches below the surface, or see them disappear into pure, pale sand. These are the kinds of soils you get when your garden has spent only the last few eons above the level of the sea. Soil conditioners and fertilizers are topics of lively discussion at parties attended by South Florida gardeners.

Yes, there's an art to gardening in South Florida. But gardeners, being gardeners, need only add a little knowledge to their natural enthusiasm to make their slices of South Florida

bloom. *The Art of South Florida Gardening* is
meant to give you that knowledge. On
its pages, you will find information
to help you plan your landscape for a South Florida
lifestyle, and to choose,
plant, and care for sub-
tropical trees and shrubs.
You'll learn how to grow a
great lawn, create a hedge,
train a tree, sculpt a shrub,
and produce the best-tasting
subtropical fruit.

You'll find the proper ways to water—and
conserve water—and to use fertilizers and pest-
control chemicals. You'll learn what to do before and after a hurricane or freeze, and how
to make a fallen tree stand up and grow again.
Those who love gardening for the table will
learn how to grow a successful South Florida
vegetable garden when it's snowing up north.

The Art of South Florida Gardening is
full of useful tips, facts, and answers to the
questions most frequently asked of Harold
Songdahl, one of South Florida's most respected horticulturists—as well as a few of his and
Millie Songdahl's favorite South Florida garden recipes. Because many South Florida gardeners find they wish to explore more fully a
particular aspect of subtropical gardening, at
the end of the book you'll find a resource list
of gardening equipment, government services,
some beautiful and educational gardens to
visit, and excellent gardening and landscaping books.

While for clarity of communication, *The
Art of South Florida Gardening* mentions specific plants and their habits, and types and
sometimes brand names of fertilizers and garden chemicals, nothing in this book should be
read as a recommendation to purchase or use

any specific plant or product. Similarly, while gardening philosophies and methods are suggested throughout the book, clearly it's up to each gardener to consider various alternatives and decide what's best for his or her situation. Think of *The Art of South Florida Gardening* as an amiable escort, as if Harold Songdahl himself were walking with you through your garden, sharing the benefits of his expertise and experience each time you open the book. The visits are always enjoyable and helpful, but ultimately, the responsibility for your garden, as well as its pleasures, belongs to you.

Even if you're an old hand at South Florida gardening, we hope you may find enjoyment in these pages. If you're new to the area, we think this book will be an indispensable guide as you plan your garden, and a valuable reference for years to come. Above all, we hope everyone who reads it will be able to apply to their own gardens the spirit of fun with which it was conceived and written. Gardening may not be for wimps, especially in hard-digging, fast-growing, hot-enough-to-fry-your-tomatoes South Florida, but while it can sometimes be hard work, it should never be a chore. And your garden should always be a haven of serenity between bouts of mowing and hedge trimming. So hook up the hammock, pour yourself a nice tall frosty glass of key limeade, and relax as you read. There'll be plenty of time to pull the weeds later.

Before You Plant, Plan

hen it comes to landscaping, most people just plant, and plant, and plant. It's understandable, really: Planting is the fun part. Gardeners love to browse up and down the rows of flowers and bushes at the local garden center, picking out the ones they want for their own yards—and in fact this is an excellent way to research what's available and become familiar with it all.

But the pick-and-plant method is not sufficient to ensure a successful landscape. Some plants that attract you may quickly outgrow the space you imagine for them. Others may have special requirements or problems you may not be aware of. While most nurseries carry plants intended for local gardens, some of the plants displayed in popular mass-merchandisers' garden departments won't even grow in the subtropics. The store's buyer may work in an office in Pittsburgh or Atlanta, and could know less about South Florida gardening than you do. That's why it's a good idea to do your browsing in nurseries established to serve South Florida, and then, if you wish, shop around for the best prices before you buy.

In any case, if before you spend money,

you make a plan, you can almost certainly prevent a lot of wasted energy and time (years, in the case of a badly chosen tree), and some costly mistakes.

Why landscape?

Even the garden of the most relaxed and spontaneous kind of person, who doesn't put much store in making elaborate plans, can benefit from being more than a random assemblage of pretty plants.

Landscaping can enhance the looks of an attractive house, or conceal the shortcomings of a less-than-perfect one. Ask any realtor: A good landscape nearly always increases the property's value. In fact, some realtors say, you can usually judge a house by its landscape. If the yard is attractive and well looked after, chances are the house will be, too. If the yard looks neglected, when you open the door, you'd better stand back.

It may also be of interest that landscaping is tax-effective. Any addition you make to your house (pools, screen rooms, driveways, barbecues) requires a permit—for which you're charged a fee. And if the improvement increases the assessed value of your house, you'll see it reflected in the next year's property taxes.

But you can landscape to your heart's content. No fee permits are required, and no additional taxes are assessed.

While complicated landscapes may best be left to the experts, simple, straightforward ones are quite easy to plan. And interesting. Nor should a plan restrict you or your creative impulses. It's meant as a guide only, with plenty of room for spontaneity along the way.

Your garden plan

If you're planning the landscape for a newly built house or one with a nice green lawn and little else, you have a clean canvas on which to work. If your house already has an established yard, you get to decide what should be removed, what to add, and how to integrate it all into something coherent, functional, and pretty enough to maybe turn a few heads. It would be wise, though, before cheerfully ripping things out, to wait and observe a well-stocked yard for four complete seasons, to see what blooms, when, and whether or not you like it. This is especially good advice for newcomers to South Florida.

Sketching it in

It's helpful to start with a more-or-less-close-to-scale drawing of your property. It need be neither fancy nor perfect. Just pace the place off (or you can use your property survey drawing) and commit its outlines to a big sheet of graph paper.

Using colored pencils or crayons to distinguish the various items, draw in your house and other buildings, cabanas, pools, patios, drives, and walkways. Shade in the slopes, if you're lucky enough to have any. This will give you a graphic representation of the relative sizes of things, which are sometimes difficult to envision, and can become an ongoing record of your activities if you sketch in plants as your garden progresses. Many gardeners find garden plans a way to crystallize the gardens they have been carrying around in their heads, and that just putting it down on paper is a satisfying first step in the actual creation.

Somewhere in the blank area that represents the house, draw a compass indicating north. The house's northern exposure will be its shady side—and in fact the house will cast a shadow of varying lengths on the yard as the sun's declination changes with the seasons—you'll notice this if you observe at different times of the year. The eastern and western sides of the house get half a day of sun each (assuming no nearby structures or shade trees), and on the south side the sun shines all day long. Knowing your house's orientation will help you decide where you'll need to plant things that will create shade, and where you can plant things that want—or won't tolerate—a lot of sun.

If you live on the Atlantic side of South Florida, make a note on the eastern margin of your drawing that the prevailing wind is from the east. On the Gulf side, the wind is from the west. This information will be useful for a number of reasons, including planning the pattern of a sprinkler system, knowing where to stake a young tree, and ensuring that thick foliage won't impede a breeze on a sultry summer evening.

Now take your plan for a walk around your property, and have a good look, up close and personal. Draw circles representing the existing trees and major shrubs you're sure you'll be keeping in the final design. Compare what you've drawn with the actual yard. Get a feel for the scale of things. If you have an open space near a property line and think a tree might be nice there, make a note—but before planting one, it's a good idea to check with the neighbors. They may love the idea of branches from your tree spreading shade over their side of the fence. On the other hand, they may be planning a vegetable garden there, and won't appreciate your tree's blocking their sun.

Don't forget to look up! Do electrical or telephone wires stretch above an easement? Sketch them in—and don't plan any tall trees there. Do you have gutters along the edges of your roof? If not, run-off from the first summer cloudburst could wipe out what you plant in its splash-path, so plan accordingly. If you know the locations of buried wires and pipes, indicate them on your plan; if you don't know, before you dig, call the utility companies to find out. More than one household in South Florida history has temporarily lost its phone lines, sewer line, TV cable, sprinkler system, or water main because of an eager-beaver gardener with a heavy shovel foot. In fact, though he doesn't admit this to everyone, Harold learned this lesson through personal experience. He cut his phone cable in three places when he built his first shade house (and the cable was two-and-a-half feet deep!).

Functions and solutions

An important step in the creation of any good garden plan is to consider what functions the landscape should perform. The front yard is the face you show the public. Good landscaping can create an inviting entrance and an attractive place for guests to park their cars. The back and side yards are typically for privacy, play, and utility (the trash cans have to go somewhere). The way you landscape these areas can create outdoor rooms for living—places to enjoy a barbecue, have a game of horseshoes, let the kids practice architecture in a sandbox, or just get away with a book to the shade of an accommodating tree. Jot some ideas on your plan. If you're an active gardener, there's no rule against reserving a spot, preferably handy to a water source, for a potting shed, a shade house, or a mist bed (learn how to build one on page 224). Even if you don't fulfill this part of the plan immediately, it'll be right there on your drawing so you can enjoy the anticipation.

Your plan can help you solve some problems, too, and screening off an unfortunate view is just the beginning. If there's a nearby school yard, highway, or shopping center you wish were a little less noisy, or road pollution you'd like to filter out, consider that bushy areca palms are excellent natural noise and dust filters. If you want to secure your property from wandering animals and other unauthorized visitors, thorny bougainvillea, natal plum, and Spanish bayonet (ouch!) can be quite persuasive. If problems like these are pertinent, make little notes in the appropriate spots on your garden plan.

Don't dig yet!

Before you rush out and start buying plants, there are still a few things to consider. Your level of commitment, for instance. Many gardeners treasure the sweaty hours they spend grubbing on all fours in the dirt, trowel in hand. Such a person would likely opt for a landscape that accommodates lots of plants. But even this kind of garden requires a disciplined basic plan to keep it from turning chaotic. This

---

How to create a sitting area outdoors

Plant three citrus trees, such as orange or tangerine or key lime, six to ten feet apart in a semi-circle around a deck or patio. As the trees grow, clean out their interior branches to about eight feet up, forming an arching canopy of interwoven branches. Decorate the trees with a few orchid plants in the Ys of the branches if you like. Arrange some comfortable outdoor chairs and tables in this leafy haven, and have a fresh limeade as you enjoy the cool, fragrant shade.

consideration should not be underestimated by working people who intend to garden primarily on weekends, because in South Florida, especially in rainy season, things can get out of hand surprisingly quickly. Even ardent gardeners can become frustrated when the heat of the sun or a torrential downpour drives them indoors before the weekend's quota of shrubs can be trimmed. You can head off problems by executing your plan slowly and methodically, an area at a time, balancing the demands of the garden against the number of hours you have to devote.

Those who admit to being less than thrilled by the idea of mowing, mulching, and dealing with the aphids out where the air conditioning doesn't reach would do well to make their landscape plans simple, to use low-maintenance plants exclusively, and to plan on hiring someone else to take care of the lawn. If you find one whose work you like, be appropriately appreciative. A good yard maintenance person is not always easy to find.

The next thing to consider is the actual design of the landscape. When people first came south to live and garden in the tropics, they imported all their ideas from other climes and cultures. For instance, even now, though most South Florida houses do not have elevated

Native or exotic?

The term "South Florida native" means a plant is indigenous to this area. But there's disagreement among the experts as to how far back to start counting. To some, the only truly native trees and shrubs are pre-Columbian—those that were growing here before the arrival of Christopher Columbus. Others accept somewhat later arrivals, brought by the natural activities of migrating birds or the processes of ocean currents or wind, that naturalized into the ecosystem.

Plants imported by humans, consciously or unconsciously, are "exotics." Much of what you see in South Florida landscapes are exotics, but, since their original habitats are similar to ours—places like South Africa, Australia, tropical South America—they usually get along beautifully with one another, as well as with native plants.

Some exotics grow and reproduce so aggressively that they choke out other plants in the process (see the official blacklist of trees on page 35). They are considered extremely undesirable and are not recommended for landscaping.

foundations, you see "foundation plantings" anyway, because that's what they had up north. European-influenced walkways had formal edgings, so formal walkway edgings appear here. A lot of houses in South Florida have perfectly respectable geometric front yards, with lawns stretching from sidewalk to fence on either side, each plot of lawn punctuated by one of a pair of matching trees. Old habits are hard to break.

The good news is that a South Florida landscaping style is coming more and more into its own, incorporating the more free-wheeling ideas of people from Caribbean and Latin American cultures, as well as those of landscape architects and laid-back long-time Florida residents.

The result is a kind of landscaping philosophy that brings our gardens into harmony with our outdoorsy way of life, and makes the most of the plant materials at our disposal. It's free-form, natural looking, and full of native plants and trees mixed in with the exotics.

Xeriscaping—intelligent planting using more drought-resistant trees and shrubs—is also increasing in popularity.

Although of course you'll want your garden to be uniquely your own, nothing in the rule book says you can't borrow some ideas from the garden down the street. Garden snooping, especially in interestingly landscaped neighborhoods like some in Coral Gables, Hobe

Slopes save water

In some of the newer residential areas, man-made hills were designed to slope away from houses, so rainwater can run into the grassy areas between them. In others, the swales between sidewalk and street are slightly bowled to guide run-off water down through the soil.

These run-off areas do more than keep rainwater away from houses and pavement. As the water sinks through the soil, it's filtered, purified, and absorbed back into the Biscayne Aquifer, South Florida's underground water supply, from which our fresh water comes.

Water not recaptured and filtered through the soil goes into the streets, down storm sewers, and, wasted, out into the bay. Flattening or filling these areas defeats their purpose, and could create a flood zone for you or your neighbors.

Sound, Sarasota, or Naples, is invaluable research. As with any art, the more you expose yourself to good landscaping, the better your own will be. While you're looking, here are a few thoughts to guide you:

From the outside in

Instead of hemming the house with shrubbery and surrounding it with an apron of grass, the new South Florida landscaping starts at the edges of your property and works inward toward the house, with interesting mixtures of foliage in curvilinear patterns, interspersed with lawn areas or not, according to the neighborhood. In Coconut Grove, the oldest section of Miami, you can find houses whose whole front yards are virtual forests of live oaks, and where ferns and other shade-loving plants take the place of grass among the trees.

Balance and scale

Landscape plants should be in scale—with your house, the size of your property, the neighborhood, one another. You'd think it would be obvious (though there's still evidence to the contrary) that an avenue of 60-foot royal palms that looks sensational on a boulevard in Palm Beach would look somewhat strange leading to the front door of a modest single-family house. But relax the straight line into more natural groupings, and the same idea could be translated into a more human scale with parotis, coconut, or queen palms.

It's usually best to work with the topography you're given. Even in South Florida,

Privacy with a view

When planting for privacy around a screened-in porch or pool enclosure, many people make the mistake of putting tall, bushy shrubs right up against the screen—effectively eliminating the rest of the yard from view.

Instead, why not plant your shrubs and trees at the property line, and surround the screening with lower plants? That way, you can lounge privately by the pool and still survey your entire kingdom.

Pathfinding

Avoid the temptation to plot a pathway that has a lot of cute angles and curves. You'll soon learn, from the trampled grass, that people will frustrate you by walking where the path *should* be. Better to keep the sweep of a path broad and smooth.

Trees as nature intended

Planting a row of trees risks the possibility that, if one dies, you'll have the landscaping equivalent of a smile with a missing tooth. Natural looking groupings or staggered semi-circles—of three, five, or any odd number—are usually more visually pleasing.

although you may find the relative flatness a bit of a yawn, unless you're a skilled expert landscape architect, the rule generally applies.

Some people think they can improve on the situation by building berms—man-made hillocks—in front of their houses. You often see large versions of these around hospitals, office buildings, and other institutions (if they are badly proportioned you may wonder if someone has buried a tank). Berms are said to help screen a house from the sight and sound of traffic, and they can be esthetically effective if well done. But beware. Berms usually present more cons than pros.

• Berms are very hard to mow, so are best planted with shrubbery or ground covers rather than grass. Even then, if not looked after, they invariably degenerate into weed patches.

• Berms dry out before the rest of your yard, so if you don't take care to plant drought-tolerant plants, additional irrigation will almost inevitably be needed.

• A good berm alternative might be a small grove of trees, a specimen flowering tree surrounded by complementary shrubs, or, a large boulder nestled in clusters of bromeliads—planted right on level ground.

Coloring it in

Every landscape is a composition of shapes and textures and colors, and this is nowhere more true than in the tropics, where multitudes of all three are available in abundance. Beautiful trees with sculptural limbs give strength to the composition. There are shrubs with big spiky leaves, slender grassy leaves, rounded leaves, heart-shaped leaves, tiny leaves, enormous showy leaves, colorful leaves, and leaves in every conceivable shade of green —some striped or splotched or bordered in contrasting hues.

You'll find flowering gingers, ixoras, gardenias, bougainvillea, hibiscus, allamanda, crossandra, birds of paradise, plumbago, jasmine, oleander, and scores of other shrubs that flower, some in their season, others throughout the year, not to mention the fabulous flowering trees that come into bloom in a year-round parade. One of a gardener's deepest satisfactions comes from learning to use these riches effectively.

In most gardens, you find more than plants. Depending on the size of the property, an area might be punctuated by a gazebo or piece of sculpture. Coral rock boulders or a twist of cyprus driftwood can create an interesting background for a collection of bromeliads. Vines can cascade over wood fences and rock walls. River rock or pine bark mulch can pave paths and swaths to link planted areas. Pools can be surrounded by bricks, tiles, keystone pavers, or wood decks.

Every garden wants a body of water, even if it's no larger than a birdbath. If you can manage a small pond or stone fountain, so much the better. For tips on water gardens, see page 196.

All this should be sketched in with pencil on your garden plan, to remind you of the requirements and possibilities. You can edit and revise as your garden develops.

Like good landscapes everywhere, a South Florida garden is an investment, not just of money, but of time, thought, energy, and heart.

Gardening in a nutshell

A gardener's enthusiasm does not necessarily grow or shrink with the size of the garden. Some of the loveliest spots in the great outdoors are as petite as patios and townhouse terraces. Usually furniture is involved—a lunch table and chairs, or a couple of chaises, or maybe there's just enough space to swing a hammock. Patios and terraces, perhaps even more than the larger gardens of single-family houses, can truly be outdoor rooms.

The only rule for patio gardens is: Keep it simple. Small spaces are very easy to mess up. Sometimes it's helpful to think of such a small space as if it were an atrium or even a dish garden, which can be charming when done correctly, and chaos if overdone.

Because space is at a premium, it is doubly important to know what each plant you're considering will look like when it's full-grown, and to be very selective about what you plant. Some gardeners keep all their patio plants in movable pots. This helps contain plants that might otherwise spread too quickly, like ginger and bamboo, and pots are invaluable if you want to rearrange.

Patios can be dramatic showcases for plant collections. Under a single tree or a trellis for shade, stunning arrangements can be created with

But don't drink it...

If you slip a few coffee filters into the bottom of a flowerpot to cover the hole before you fill the pot with soil, water will drain through, but the soil won't.

Imports in pots

If you like to experiment, a big pot full of good soil can be a practical place to do it. Some South Florida gardeners have reported surprising success with northern plants and seeds, by growing them in the carefully controlled environment of a pot.

A gem of a gel

If you dislike watering, or you travel a lot, you might want to try adding polymer gel crystals to your potting soil. Soak them in water first according to directions; expanded, the crystals hold up to 20 times their volume. Add the expanded gel to the soil as instructed, so it can release the water gradually into the soil. Treated pots, and even plants in the ground, can go for weeks before they need watering again.

If you invest wisely and well, the return will be a garden that grows lovelier and more rewarding as the years pass.

bromeliads and orchids. A terrace wall or fence is tailor-made for hanging ferns or mounting pots of miniature roses. Pedestals of varying heights can display a bonsai collection.

Remember that many patios and terraces tend to be shady, and especially so after you've brought in even a small tree in a tub. But there are lots of plants that will thrive in the shade, and some, if you select carefully, will stay beautiful for 20 years in the same pot. Nor need you be without color. Many shade-loving foliage plants sport colorful leaves, and the crimsons, purples, peaches, and pinks of impatiens, South Florida's best-selling annual flower, can gleam like jewels in hanging baskets or spilling from pots down on the flagstones.

Branching into Trees

very garden needs a tree. Even if your yard is tiny, you can nearly always find a spot for a small tree for architectural scale. Trees add the visual interest of leafy light and shadow, create privacy, can produce fruit or flowers, and make cooling shade for a hammock, a picnic table, a south-facing window, or an air conditioner.

Trees clean the air, inhaling the carbon dioxide exhaled or coughed into the atmosphere during the day by humans, animals, and the exhausts of internal combustion engines, and exchanging it for the oxygen we need to live. That's why forest air is so sweet and fresh, and why it's so delicious to sleep among trees. It's also why, each time you plant a tree, you're doing something good for the earth. Wise gardeners have as many trees as they can within the constraints of their property size and garden plans.

They also plant their trees first—not only because the trees help anchor and define planting areas, making the rest of the landscape that much easier to visualize, but for the plain, practical reason that trees take longest to grow. For this same reason, full-grown trees are the most valuable plants in a landscape.

Mature trees—even the ones you might not have chosen yourself—are working for you, adding grace and character and a look of establishment to your house and garden. If you were spotted energetically ripping out a hedge or some philodendrons or the last owner's amaryllis collection, nobody would be particularly bothered. But it's rare that anyone would, without first doing some serious thinking (and checking regulations), cut down a tree.

It is nevertheless a mistake to suppose that all trees are desirable in a garden setting. Ficus trees, marvelous looking as they are with their immense canopies and tropical tangles of aerial roots that spread the tree ever wider—were at one time planted too close to houses. Now, having done what comes naturally over the decades, many have overgrown their welcome. Norfolk Island pines (ersatz pines at that), are really too tall and brittle for most good landscaping. And trees like Brazilian pepper and melaleucas are allergenic and hostile to the landscape—weeds of the tree family—and should be eliminated. Some trees will get the ax for esthetic or other reasons. They're badly placed, badly damaged, diseased, or just not to your liking.

To chop or not to chop

State and county regulatory authorities require that you get permission before cutting down a tree of a given size (in Dade County, for example, one that measures more than 18 inches across at chest height). In many wetland environments, the federal government has a say, too. Some trees are totally protected; even trimming them isn't allowed (mangroves, for example). And many communities prohibit hat-rack pruning of trees. The appropriate authority will have the latest regulations. Ignorance of the law is not considered an excuse, and you can get into real trouble for truncating a tree.

When choosing a tree, it's important to consider its eventual size. Trees that grow large (30 feet and above) should be planted well away from the house. No big tree should be planted closer than 10 feet to a house, drive, or walkway. Palms and small, decorative trees that look nice punctuating clusters of shrubs should still be kept

at least five feet away. As for ficus trees, Harold's rule is that they should never be planted closer than 400 feet from any structure. Period. Experience has shown that even though a tree's roots aren't likely to jack up a house (though they can lift a sidewalk), if planted too near the house the tree won't be able to grab well on that side, making it less stable, and therefore less likely to withstand a stiff wind.

If you're looking for the perfect tree, you are going to be disappointed. Every kind of tree is apt to have some habit or characteristic that, if you'd been in charge of its design, you'd have corrected. Some are shallow rooted, making them easy prey for a gale. Others' roots won't think twice about invading your sprinkler pipes, septic tank, or sewer line, through the tiniest available crack. Some trees are dense, giving too much shade and keeping out the breeze. Some are rigid and stilted looking. Some drop enormous leaves that will pile up on your lawn—or annoying little fruits that muck up the pavement and perfume the air with aromas only a fruit fly could love.

The tree to choose is the one with the most positives and the least negatives for your situation. Though you'll find on these pages the names and characteristics of some of Harold's favorite shade, flowering, fruit, and palm trees, there are far too many for the list to be comprehensive. Because of this, it's well worth your time and effort to do some first-hand research before making a purchase. You might look at a few illustrated books, visit public gardens in your area, and seek out growers who specialize in the sorts of trees you're considering: flowering trees, native trees, fruit trees, palms. Take *The Art of South Florida Gardening* with you as a prompt to help you ask the right questions.

Trees for shade

If shade is what you're after, and nothing but shade will do, there are lots of classic, no-nonsense, leafy trees to choose from. Here are a few good ones:

Live oak (*Quercus virginiana*). If you can have only one shade tree, make it a live oak. If you have space for more than one, so much the better. The stateliest tree of all, a live oak will give your landscape the grace and dignity of old Florida. Unlike northern oaks, live oaks are not deciduous, but continually produce and drop their leaves, which filter unobtrusively into the surrounding greenery.

Their roots penetrate deeply, and their branches form a good scaffolding with lots of character. In the wild, live oak branches are found covered with orchids and bromeliads. In the garden, they could be, too. Live oaks are native throughout the state.

Black olive (*Bucida buceras*).
Though black olives are not black and
will never produce an olive, they are big,
beautiful, fast growing, and therefore very
popular. Black olive trees tend to drop sticky,
staining flowers, making them a poor choice
near driveways where they can make a target
of the roof of your car. Black olives are native
to the upper Keys.

Gumbo limbo (*Bursera simaruba*). This
tree, whose name may make you feel like dancing, is also called the sunburn tree because of
its peeling reddish skin. You can create an instant gumbo limbo tree by sticking a sawn-off
limb—a big one, with branches—in the ground
and keeping it watered until it sprouts.

Gumbo limbo is known in Cuba as the
living fence because its branches are used as
fence posts, which used to take root and grow
into trees. To prevent this, clever fence builders finally hit upon the idea of installing their
branches upside down. Native from Key West
to Cape Canaveral and Bradenton.

Allspice tree (*Pimenta dioica*). Medium-sized native tree with stiff, seven-
inch aromatic leaves used for making bay
rum. Its tiny 1/4-inch fruit, called allspice,
is used in cooking, and, Harold can attest,
also brews into quite a tasty liqueur.

Paradise tree (*Simarouba glauca*).
Large evergreen tree dense with compound
leaves (and messy fruit and seeds). Native
from Cape Canaveral south, including the
Naples area.

**Podocarpus (*Podocarpus
macrophyllus*).** The very same plants you see
pruned as cones, spheres, and pillars by
people's front doors, and as thick, sharp-cor-
nered hedges, can also be grown, with a little
judicious shaping, as small-to-medium multi-
trunked, evergreen, shaggy-leaved shade trees.

Mahogany (*Swietenia mahagoni*). A large, handsome tree with small, fluttery compound leaves. Native to upper Keys and Cape Sable, and alas, according to experts, somewhat prone to disease when planted too far from home.

Tamarind (*Lysiloma latisiliqua*). A medium-sized tree with feathery compound leaves. Produces edible sticky brown fruit that makes your mouth pucker, but that can be used to make tasty drinks and chutneys. Native to Keys and mainland hammocks.

Satin leaf (*Chrysophyllum oliviforme*). A lovely medium-sized tree whose leaves are shiny green with coppery undersides. Native to South Florida hammocks.

Silver buttonwood (*Conocarpus erectus*). A charming tree with small leaves of pale, silvery green. Native to South Florida, and found in the wild at hammock edges and on the landward side of mangroves, the fuzzy-leafed silver buttonwood has shown a distinct preference for gardens near the sea (the salt air discourages a blackening fungus that preys on it). A more recently developed smooth-leafed variety called Silver Sheen is more resistant to this fungus, and can be planted with confidence further inland.

Red maple (*Acer rubrum*). A good-sized tree whose leaves are of the classic northern maple-leaf shape in two-tone green. The leaves even turn red and yellow in the fall. Cold-tolerant, native to Florida, but requires lots of water.

Flowering trees

The philosophy of flowering trees, judging by the shows they put on periodically, is if you've got it, flaunt it. Then, after they've finished flaunting, many become delightful green shade trees until the next performance.

The only drawback to these stars of the arboreal world is that they can by nature be rather untidy. It's the price we pay for all that glory. Best to put them center stage in the middle of the yard, or on the swale right in front of the footlights, so the flowers, leaves, and pods can fall through filtering foliage plants beneath, or on the grass where you can admire the pools of glowing petals before you mow them up.

Many landscapers have noticed that, once established, some subtropical flowering trees appear to bloom more vigorously when kept on the dry side once they've reached maturity. This makes them good choices for for areas not supplied by the irrigation system. It may also be the answer to the exasperating question of why flowering trees can be seen blooming their heads off on roadway median strips where nobody seems to even bother to water them.

Small- to medium-sized flowering trees (up to 20 feet high), while gorgeous as singular specimens, are also very effective when planted in informal mini-groves of three or five—an odd number always looks best— planted five or six feet apart so their branches will intertwine as they grow.

Larger trees (30 feet tall and up) might feel hemmed in if you planted more than one in the average-sized yard. But if you have a big enough property, five or seven of any tree—even the huge poinciana or jacaranda trees—planted in staggered combinations 10 to 20 feet apart, will eventually create a beautiful blended canopy above a multiple-trunked grove.

Most flowering trees bloom once a year, usually for four or five weeks. Some bloom several times or continually throughout the year, but their flowers might not be as showy.

Many flowering trees are deciduous, meaning they lose most of their leaves for part of the year in preparation for their annual display. This is not necessarily a bad thing. Apart from the visual sensation of a tree completely enrobed in flowers without the distraction of greenery, the leaves usually drop conveniently in the cooler months, when the milder sun is welcome on your lawn or patio; in summer, when you want shade, the leaves are agreeably lush. Also, if a tree drops its leaves all at once, you have to clean them up only once. Most of the bauhinia orchid trees, for example, do this. But one variety, *Bauhinia blakeana* or Hong Kong orchid tree, drops flowers, leaves, pods, twigs, and anything else it has on hand, all year long. Some people are willing to put up with this in return for 12 months of nonstop bloom. Others aren't. Here are a few favorite flowering trees:

Royal poinciana (*Delonix regia*). Red-orange blooms in spring, as quickly as three years after planting (but it could take 14). Grows from seed, but faster-flowering grafted trees are available. Can easily grow to 60 feet tall, with a spreading umbrella-like canopy of high branches and soft, lacy leaves. Harold calls these trees "self-pruning," which means the lower limbs have a tendency to drop off as the tree grows. If you'd prefer the look of a poinciana, only in yellow, nature has graciously obliged by creating the brilliant *Peltephorum pterocarpum*, or copper pod.

Frangipani or plumeria (*Plumeria acuminata*). A decorative tree that blooms in spring, often less than a year after planting. Its richly fragrant flowers—white, yellow, pink, blends, or deep red, are used in Hawaiian leis. They appear in clusters on branches that are typically bare and sculpturelike during the dry season. Grows from large cuttings, and reaches as tall as 40 feet, but can be kept shorter.

Queen's crape myrtle (*Lagerstroemia speciosa*). Not the crape myrtle shrub, but a spectacular tree that can grow 30 or 40 feet tall, with rough oblong leaves that turn autumn colors before they drop for the winter. Crowned in spring with luxurious clusters of large frilly violet to indigo blossoms (there is a white variety, but it is more rare). Native of India. Can bloom in as few as two years.

Jacaranda (*Jacaranda acutifolia*). The classic jacaranda has clusters of lavender-blue blooms in spring (there's a magenta variety, too), and delicate feathery leaves. Grafted ones can bloom in two or three years; non-grafted trees take as long as seven to 14. An Amazon native, it can grow to 50 feet tall.

Pink trumpet tree (*Tabebuia pallida*). Has flowers ranging from white to deep rose, appearing heavily in spring, more sparsely at other times during the year. About 25 feet tall, blooms two or three years after planting. An excellent swale tree.

Golden showers (*Cassia fistula*). Has light green compound leaves and panicles of bright yellow flowers in spring. Blooms within a few years after planting; can grow as tall as 40 feet.

Weeping bottlebrush (*Callistemon viminalis*). A tree with elegant twisty limbs and bottle-brush-shaped flowers of red or magenta that keep coming pretty much all year. Once it starts blooming, it usually blooms profusely the first five years, then tapers off. Grows about 30 feet tall. Epiphytes like to cling to its rough bark.

Tree of gold (*Tabebuia caraiba [argentea]*). A smallish, rather unprepossessing tree most of the year, that suddenly bursts into incredibly rich golden bloom in spring. Usually devoid of its slender pale green leaves when in bloom, making it even more magnificent. Tends to evelop dramatic twists and gnarls as it grows. Good for cluster planting. Cats love to climb its corklike bark.

Lancepod (*Lonchocarpus violaceous*). A lovely small tree about 20 feet tall, with violet flowers reminiscent of sweet-peas appearing in October. Usually blooms within a couple of years of planting, and its leaves that remain green and plentiful most of the year. Harold calls it the Trinidad lilac.

Silk floss tree (*Chorisia speciosa*). In autumn, big flowers of white, pink, or deep rose appear, followed by seed pods like fluffy pompons, giving this tree its nickname. Recognizable by the interesting-looking large, blunt thorns on its trunk. Grows 40 feet tall.

Jerusalem thorn tree (*Parkinsonia aculeata*). Thorny branches are bare in winter, covered in spring with thousands of tiny yellow flowers, followed by needlelike leaves. About 20 feet tall, it blooms in two or three years, and has a life span of about 15.

Geiger (*Cordia sebestena*). A native, upright grower about 20 feet tall, with sandpapery leaves, bright orange flowers, and edible fruit. Safest planted south of Homestead because of its sensitivity to freezes. Comes with its own beetle—the jewel-like tortoise beetle. Its cousin is the **white geiger (*Cordia boissieri*)**, a Texas native with similarly sandpapery leaves and clusters of crinkly white flowers. The white geiger is evergreen, has a bushier, more rounded silhouette, and is less sensitive to the cold than the orange geiger. Both kinds of geiger bloom year round.

Fruit trees

South Florida is one of the premier places on earth in which to grow tropical fruit trees. In fact, this may be one of the reasons you decided to move here.

Some fruit trees are exotic and rare, like the jaboticaba tree, with sweet, small, plum-like fruits that grow along its branches. Rarity has its price, however. Less rare, but still quite out of the ordinary and likely to dazzle visitors from up north, are trees like the carambola, which produces sweet-and-sour yellow fruit that forms stars when you slice it; the black sapote (*Diospyros digyna*) or chocolate pudding tree, with large, sweet, brown fruits; or the hurricane-resistant sapodilla, or chicle (*Manilkara zapota*)—a big, handsome tree with glossy leaves, whose brown fruit contains extremely sweet tan-colored edible pulp, and whose sap was originally used for making chewing gum.

Papaya's little girl

Only the female papaya bears edible fruit, and the only way to tell a male from a female is by the tree's blossoms. The male's flowers bloom on long racemes that are lovely in arrangements.

The female's single flattened bell-shaped blossoms appear above the leaf joints just before the fruit begins to form.

There are also bi-sex papayas, which have both kinds of flowers, and will bear fruit. The significance of all this is that if you try to grow papaya trees from seeds, you won't know until they blossom whether they're papayas or mamayas.

Papayas in the bag

If you discover fruit flies hanging around your papayas, you can expect grubs in the fruit where the flies have laid their eggs. To get the papayas before they do, as soon as the fruits appear, slip gallon-size plastic bags over them, poke a few air holes, and tie at the stem with twist-ties. Leave the bags on until the papayas mature and ripen. You can use the same technique with any fruit that's prone to attract flies.

If you have a large enough yard, consider a good old-fashioned mulberry tree. They're tall trees with generous canopies, and are too messy to sit under, but they produce lots of tasty berries. When Harold was a kid, he and his chums found the low-branching, easily climbed scaffolding of a mulberry tree the perfect playhouse in which to spend their summer vacations, with tongues, lips, and fingers perpetually purple.

Some fruit trees, like the banana and the easy-to-grow papaya tree (whose ripe fruit is marvelous diced and chilled with key-lime juice and maybe a dash of sugar) are not really trees at all, but overgrown herbs. That's why they need so much water, and why they're so susceptible to cold. Still, it's nice to have a stand of papayas or a cluster of banana trees back in the corner, in a low spot that tends to stay moist. Banana trees are especially heavy eaters, so be sure to toss your ravenous clump a couple of handfuls of fertilizer at least once a month. Mature banana trees can grow anywhere from six to 30 feet tall, and they're very tropical looking. Don't forget that coconuts are fruits, too (containing very large seeds), and that a coconut palm is the quintessential tropical-looking tree.

Mostly, though, when people think of growing fruit in South Florida, they think of three kinds: mango, avocado, and citrus.

When to pickabanana

As a banana stalk matures, the bananas will first plump, then ripen. Typically, bananas are not allowed to ripen on the tree. Instead, when the upper-most (oldest) hand of bananas shows a trace of yellow, the entire stalk is cut and hung in the shade, protected from rain. Harold, however, often lets the bananas ripen on the tree, picking them —or letting the kids have the fun of picking them—as they become ready to eat.

When to thinabanana

If your banana grove starts delivering poor yields, the trees may be too crowded. Crowded banana trees must compete with one another for fertilizer, and may end up not having sufficient energy reserves to set fruit. Try thinning them to four feet apart, and see if they don't do better next season.

Mango mania

If you ask an American to name the most popular fruit in the world, he'd probably guess wrong. Mangos, along with bananas, are consumed by more people around the globe than any other fruit, by a wide margin. If you plant a mango tree, you might happily become part of the statistics.

Mature mango trees are quite substantial, easily 30 or 40 feet tall. They come in many varieties (you can see more than 100 at South Florida's Mango Forum, an annual grower-sponsored event) and most are well suited to private gardens. Nearly all mangos taste voluptuously good (try them sliced liberally—OK, wantonly—into vanilla ice cream), but each is unique. They all look different, too: Some are golden yellow; some pink as an Easter egg; others rainbow blends. So before you decide which variety to plant, you owe yourself a taste test. Fruit tree specialists usually have more than one variety of mango for sale, and will often let you taste the fruit if it's in season.

Coralee's ridiculously easy mango pie

Cut into bite-size chunks as many ripe, juicy mangos as needed to fill a baked pie shell. Top with freshly whipped cream or a layer of softened vanilla ice cream or frozen yogurt. Decorate with mango slices.

A favorite—and the standard to which other mangoes are often compared—is the Haden, which has wonderful rosy color and great flavor and texture. Its crop size can be inconsistent from year to year, though, and it seems more susceptible than most to attacks by anthrachnose fungus. Other good mangos are Kent, Keitt, Zill, and the small but very tasty Carrie. Each variety has a different season, so if you're mad about mangoes and have the space, you could plant one of each of several kinds and have mangoes practically all year long. Be sure to keep plenty of vanilla ice cream (or, all right, fat-free frozen yogurt) on hand.

Avocadissimo

Let's get one thing straight: When South Floridians say "avocado," we're not talking about those mean little bumpy things they grow in California. Florida avocados are big and plump and buttery, luscious in salads and sandwiches and guacamole, and great filled with shrimp or crab salad or just eaten with a spoon "on the half shell," as Harold likes to say, maybe with a sprinkle of salt and coarse ground pepper, or a drizzle of good olive oil.

These big avocados grow on big trees, commonly 30 feet tall and 30 feet across. As with mangos, there are so many kinds of avocados that it's smart to go to a specialist nursery and be guided by an expert—and your own taste buds. Some of the most widely planted varieties: Choquette, Hall, Simmons, Pollock, Monroe, the old-fashioned Lula, and Fairchild, with its tender fruit and peel flashed with eggplant-purple when ripe. As with mangos, different kinds of avocados bear at different times of year.

You'll hear in some tree circles that avocados must be planted in pairs—A and B types—in order to get themselves pollinated and set fruit. Don't overly concern yourself with this. There are enough avocado trees in

---

Harold's not-quite-guacamole

Chop a ripe avocado into a bowl. Add salt, pepper, and Tabasco sauce, and mix it all up into a chunky goo. Serve with tortilla chips.

The old avocado-pit trick

Sure you can grow an avocado tree from an avocado pit (and a mango tree from a mango pit). Don't bother rooting it on the windowsill first, put it right in the ground or in a pot of soil. You may have to wait as long as 14 years for fruit (then again you might not), and the fruit may not be an exact copy of the fruit you got the pit from, (but then again, it might just turn out to be better). Harold's neighbor planted the pit from one of Harold's avocados. It bore fruit in three years and was, Harold attests, the most delicious avocado he ever tasted: "Better than the parent."

South Florida that most have little trouble finding a date. To be sure about the varieties you're considering, check with a specialist grower.

Avocado trees cannot live with soggy bottoms, so be sure to plant yours where drainage is good. Fungus can sometimes be a problem, and the trees can be attacked by rust, a lower form of plant life (which does no harm to the fruit, however). And caterpillars may shred the leaves and birds will want to share the fruit. If you're a purist or a commercial grower, you'll want to spray regularly with copper for the rust and to keep as much as possible of the fruit on the tree. You'll also go after the worms with an appropriate pesticide. Harold doesn't bother with any of this. Even if you lose some of your crop to fungus and birds, he says, not to worry. There'll be plenty left from a healthy tree for you, your extended family, and most of your neighbors.

The juice on citrus

When people move to South Florida, they usually want a citrus tree. This may at first be prompted by a desire to send their friends back home photos of themselves out on their patios in the middle of winter, eating grapefruit and drinking orange juice from their own trees while their friends scrape ice from their windshields. The smug satisfaction can be nearly as sweet as the fruit itself.

Citrus trees usually run in the 20-foot range, making them ideal for group plantings —though grapefruit and key lime trees have been known to grow to 30 feet tall. Some excellent citrus choices:

Temple orange. Easy to peel, tastes great, few seeds, good for eating out of hand.

Valencia orange. The sweetest orange of all. A few more seeds than the Temple, but probably worth it.

Tangerine. Larger than the supermarket kind, almost seedless, very sweet.

Minneola tangelo (known as Honeybell at the supermarkets). A cross between a tangerine and a grapefruit, tangelos are excellent eaten out of hand. They're also very sweet and make tasty juice.

Marsh seedless grapefruit. Sweet and easy to eat. Also try other pink or red varieties.

Duncan grapefruit. A lovely flavor but full of seeds.

Key lime. Often called Mexican limes outside of Florida, these little limes are grown around the world, far more abundantly than the more familiar (to Americans) Persian limes. Persian limes, incidentally, are native to Tahiti, and are therefore really Tahitian limes, which is what they were called when Harold was a kid.

Key limes are typically small, round, yellow, and tart, and usually grow in clusters on an attractive tree. They make excellent limeade (just squeeze a Key lime into a tall glass, add sugar, ice, and water), and, of course, South Florida's most famous dessert, key lime pie.

Before long, we may find ourselves with a whole new generation of citrus trees to grow. Thanks to the dedicated gene-splicers

---

Millie Songdahl's Key Lime Pie

Lightly beat 6 egg yolks with a fork (reserve whites). Add one can sweetened condensed milk, and mix thoroughly.

Slowly blend in 1/2 cup freshly squeezed key lime juice—about five or six limes. As juice is added, mixture will "cook" and thicken. Pour into baked pie shell (some people use a graham cracker crust) and refrigerate.

Beat 6 egg whites with about 3 Tbs. sugar until stiff peaks form. Spread meringue over pie. Bake in 350° oven until meringue is golden.

Lime ice

Key lime juice can be frozen in ice-cube trays and stored in plastic zip-lock bags until you need them for iced tea. They also give cola drinks a nice nip.

The color of oranges

- The oranges that grow on the outer branches of a tree tend to color to a more intense orange because they get more sun. The more interior oranges of equal maturity will typically have the same quality and flavor, even if they appear more green.

- But don't be too quick to pick. Citrus fruit does not ripen once it's off the tree.

- To test for an orange's ripeness, feel it. If it's plump, peel and taste it. If it tastes good, the rest of the oranges on the tree will be good, too.

- Cold weather intensifies the glow of an orange's cheeks, and will also make it sweeter.

- The russeting commonly seen on dooryard oranges is caused by a tiny rust mite. It affects the skin only, and, contrary to citrus mythology, does not make the fruit any sweeter.

on the cutting edge of horticultural science, more and more kinds of citrus will be available without annoying seeds to contend with.

Even more interesting, actual new kinds of fruit are making their debuts. Among the most recent arrivals is the **ambersweet**—half orange, 3/8 tangerine, and 1/8 grapefruit, but known for simplicity as an orange—which produces an extraordinarily flavorful juice.

Going for the graft

If you take a seed from the half-grapefruit you're eating and push it into a pot full of soil, chances are it will grow. It may, in time, become a respectable-looking tree. Eventually, this tree may even bear fruit (though it may not). But the probability is very high that you'll wait several years to find out whether it will bear, and, if it does, the type and quality of its fruit. Of course, it can be fun to grow a seed—and interesting. Years ago, two college students doing an experiment collected the rogue seeds from some hybrid seedless limes, planted them, and wound up with, not lime trees, but lots of *different* kinds of citrus.

The original seedless lime trees had been pollinated by insects that had not been fussy about which trees they visited.

If you're serious about growing a citrus tree, it's a far better idea to buy a grafted tree —part of a mature fruiting branch grafted onto selected rootstock—which, typically, will blossom and begin bearing the sort of fruit you bargained for within a couple of years.

It also pays to buy your trees at a specialist fruit tree nursery. The people there are experts. They work closely with their trees, and can tell you all about them. Many will happily tell you more than you ever wished to know. Patient listening is often rewarded with generous samples of luscious fruit. Some of these nurseries are located in interesting areas, getting you out into parts of South Florida you may not otherwise have thought of visiting.

Once at the nursery, you may find yourself confronted with a choice between a robust little plant in a conventional three-gallon can and a rather spindly excuse for a tree in a strange-looking vertical cone about 16 inches tall and six inches across the top. The correct choice may surprise you: It's the cone. Its length allows the tree's tap root—which will let it tap into the underground water supply —to grow straight down, whereas inside a pot a tap root is forced into unnatural coils. Once planted, the underweight wonder will gratefully dig in and leaf out twice as fast as a similar size tree in a pot.

For nostalgic Northerners

If you miss those old fruit trees back home, be comforted. It is possible to grow varieties that do well in South Florida—though you might have to search for them, and invest some effort in their care. As Harold likes to point out, if you don't see many apple trees in your neighborhood, there's probably a reason.

If you'd like to give Northern-style trees a try, consider the Ceylon peach tree, with silvery bark and lovely pink blossoms, which produces small, tasty, freestone fruit. You'll need to protect the little peaches with plastic bags, though, because Caribbean fruit flies love them. There are tropical varieties of apple trees, too, as well as a "tropical apricot" (not a true apricot), *Dovyalis hebecarpa*. For help with your selection, you'd do well to consult a rare fruit grower.

Where to find it

Good sources for hard-to-find fruit trees are the special sales that fruit tree clubs and other horticultural organizations—rare fruit councils, the Fruit & Spice Park, and various botanical gardens around South Florida—sponsor periodically throughout the year.

Palms

Palms are probably the most tropical-looking trees in the world, as anyone who has ever watched a sunset through rustling fronds can attest. And the sound of a breeze through the fronds of a palm tree is as soothing as a waterfall.

There are many varieties of palm trees, each with its own distinctive character. Getting to know them might take a bit of time, some reading, and a few visits to specialist nurseries, but it's time well spent, and a very enjoyable pursuit.

Palmate

Pinnate

Just fronds

To get you started, palms come in two basic types: ***Palmate*** palm fronds are fan-shaped, like a hand's outspread fingers. Examples are the Washingtonia palm (*Washingtonia robusta*), European fan palm (*Chamaerops humilis*), the low-growing saw palmetto (*Serenoa repens*) seen in South Dade's pinelands, and the sable or cabbage palm (*Sabal palmetto*), native throughout most of the state, and the Florida state tree.

Pinnate palm fronds are long and featherlike. Examples are those of the tall, columnar Florida royal palm (*Roystonea elata*), native to the Collier County area, graceful queen palm (*Syagrus romanzoffiana*), bushy areca palm (*Chrysalidocarpus lutescens*), and the beautiful coconut palm (*Cocos nucifera*).

It would be possible, if you wished, to landscape your whole yard in virtually nothing but palms—using several different varieties, including triangle palms (*Neodypsis decaryi*) with their tri-cornered crowns, slow-growing pigmy date palms (*Phoenix roebelenii*), clusters of shade-loving bamboo palms (*Chamaedorea erumpens*), a fishtail palm (*Caryota mitis*), whose pinnate fronds have leaflets like dense schools of fishtails, and tall coconut palms thrusting skyward. Such gardens can be show stoppers.

Used more sparingly, palms add a touch of the tropics to any landscape. A semicircle of palms makes a protected setting for a picnic. Palms are beautiful punctuating a pool. And in the midst of a planting area or set off on the lawn, two or three palms planted together in a common hole will bow gracefully to each other as they grow.

Some palms thrive in shade. Lady palms (*Rhapis excelsa*) can be grown in clusters, and are just 10 to 15 feet tall. The dwarf variety, *Rhapis subtilis*, is even shorter. Kentia (*Howea forsteriana*), an elegant feathery palm, tolerates shade so well it even grows indoors. You usually find Kentia planted three to a tub (expensive, though. Bring your gold card). The bamboo palm is an indoor gardener's dream. It likes low light, soil on the dry side, and infrequent fertilization.

Since the pace at which most palm trees grow is relatively relaxed, the smaller varieties tend to be quite comfortable in pots, and often thrive for several years before having to be moved to a larger pot. This makes them ideal porch and patio plants. Some, like coconut palms, are salt-tolerant, thriving in beachfront landscapes.

While no tree is totally hurricane proof, palms are more resistant than most, largely owing to their flexibility. They bend with the wind and bring their fronds to a point, make them just about as slippery as a tree can manage.

One of palm trees' major advantages is that they're clean trees. Instead of dropping thousands of leaves, they shed a frond at a time. Some don't drop their fronds at all, but keep them as a flounce around the top of the trunk. This makes them excellent choices for poolside.

While some bear flowers, simply removing the spathe or boat (the large pod from which the flowers emerge) before the blooms appear prevents the mess—and you can use the flower stalk in a dried arrangement.

Some other native palms

Paurotis palm (*Acoelorrhaphe wrightii*) from Daytona Beach south

Silver palm (*Coccothrinax argentata*) Dade and Monroe Counties

Thatch palm (*Thrinax morrisii*) South Florida and the Keys

Sargent cherry palm or Buccaneer palm *(Pseudophoenix sargentii)* —the rarest palm of all. Elliott and Long Keys.

Fishtail
palm

Palms are so important to South Florida that research is always being done into the best ways to care for them. The current correct "palm special" fertilizer, for instance, has a 12-4-12 formulation, with four percent magnesium and long-lasting potash. You'll find explanations about fertilizers and their use in "Making Plants Grow— Nutrition, Nutrition, Nutrition," starting on page 101. More detailed information about fertilizing, transplanting, or in other ways caring for palms is available at the offices of your County Cooperative Extension Service. See page 240.

Hardly any insects or diseases infect palms (watch for the stinging saddleback caterpillar on some areca palms), but one palm tree killer wiped out nearly a generation of coconut and date palms in South Florida: lethal yellowing. Since its terrible invasion, palms resistant to lethal yellowing have been introduced, but there are still two kinds of palm that are easy prey; you'd be wise not to plant them. They are the Christmas palm and the Jamaican tall coconut. Resistant Malayan and Maypan coconut palms are better choices.

There are no guarantees against lethal yellowing, but resistant trees will decrease the risk. Malayan coconuts come in two interesting varieties, Malay yellow and Malay green, named for the color of their fruit and fronds. They're called "dwarf" trees, but that's because they start bearing coconuts when the trunks are only four feet tall; the tree will continue to grow as tall as any other coconut palm.

Palm trees must not be pruned the way

Palms up

Here's some new wisdom about palm nutrition:

• Special high-potash fertilizer helps keep old fronds greener longer.

• When the old fronds finally begin to turn yellow, it's best to leave them on until they're crispy. They supply vital nutrients to the rest of the tree. If you must remove them, those nutrients should be replaced by additional fertilization.

other trees are. You can take off individual fronds without doing damage, and many people like to remove the old brown fronds before they fall off. But if you remove the growing crown or tip at the top of the trunk, you'll be committing palmicide.

Clustering palms like arecas and fishtail palms can be thinned out, and the height and width of the clump adjusted, by taking out individual stalks—the tall ones or the new little ones, depending on what effect you're trying to achieve. Some people try to prune their arecas by cutting off their tops, expecting new growth to appear. It doesn't work. New growth always comes from the roots, so you may as well prune the stalks all the way to the ground.

How to plant a tree

Every science has its controversies, and horticulture is no exception. The best way to plant a tree has been, and continues to be, a subject of much debate among the experts.

Since South Florida's soils are laughably poor, traditionalists think it makes more sense to dig a hole a lot wider and deeper than the tree's root ball, discard the original soil, and replace it with a good, rich, purchased soil medium. The technical expression for this is "putting a $5 plant in a $10 hole." Proponents maintain it gives the young tree the early advantage of a solid boost of nutrition.

Modernists counter that this spares the rod and spoils the tree, encouraging its roots to stay in the hole rather than digging into the surrounding earth where they can hold on more tenaciously. This school of thought recommends breaking up the earth for several feet in every direction around the tree, but digging the hole only slightly larger than the root ball and adding just a kick of extra nutrition. Each method requires about the same amount of labor. It's up to you to decide which club you'd rather join.

When you purchase a tree, chances are it will be in a plastic pot or metal can (unless you're lucky enough to find a citrus tree in a cone).

If its root ball is wrapped in burlap, don't take the burlap off. However, when you plant the tree, be sure the burlap is completely buried. Burlap that protrudes above soil level will wick water away from the tree and dry the soil.

The traditional way:

Dig a big hole—at least several inches wider than a small pot, maybe a foot wider than a large one, and several inches deeper.

To thoroughly wet the hole and surrounding soil, fill the hole with water and let it drain. Pour in sufficient planting medium (a good quality potting mix enriched with manure, leaf mold, or other organics is fine) so that, when you lower the tree into the hole, the soil level of the root ball is level with the surrounding ground. If you must err, keep the surrounding ground lower, never higher. You can check this by laying a rake handle or straight stick across the hole.

Remove the tree from its pot, or, if the tree is heavy or stubborn, cut the pot from the root ball. If the roots are completely spiraled, slash them in two or three places around the edges, severing the long roots. This will encourage new, straight root growth outward from the trunk.

Center the tree in the hole, as straight as possible. If the tree is growing at an angle, tilt the root ball so the trunk will be vertical.

Holding the tree straight and steady, let water run slowly into the hole as you pour additional potting mix around the root ball. Don't pack the soil down; the running water will remove any air pockets while preserving the oxygen the tree needs. When planting a large tree, a professional will often plunge a digging bar into the soil and rock it back and forth all around the root ball while running a strong stream of water. This can release surprisingly large air pockets. If you run out of potting soil, back-fill with soil removed from the hole.

The modernist's way:

In rocky areas, break up the earth at least as deep as the root ball, and preferably somewhat deeper, in a large area around the spot where your tree is to be planted. You'll almost certainly need a pick-ax or digging bar to do this, and for a largish tree you might want to hire a hole digger with a big auger. In commercial South Florida groves, heavy-duty trenchers make tattersall patterns across whole fields of rocky soil before planting. They once used small charges of dynamite —no kidding. Sand gardeners can skip this step.

In the center of this loosened area, dig a hole just slightly larger than the root ball. Toss in a few handfuls of manure, set in your tree so the trunk is straight and the top of the root ball is level with the surrounding earth, and, while running water into the hole, back-fill with the soil that came out of the hole.

Watering

Remove grass and other vegetation at least two feet all the way around the tree, and build a six-inch dike of soil around the trunk to form a basin. Let water trickle in to fill this basin. Fill the basin once a day for a week, every other day for the second week, and then taper off and water as required. If you are lucky enough to have a layer of marl—Florida's swamp clay—on top of coral rock, you can water somewhat less often, since marly soil tends to hold the water longer.

Staking

Young trees should be staked. This prevents their roots from breaking if the tree shifts in the hole. For very small trees, you can just pound in a wooden tomato stake or a length of half-inch rebar (reinforcement bar used in concrete construction) on each side of the trunk, about eight inches away. If the tree seems weak, use longer stakes until it builds up some muscle and self-confidence. Using green plastic nursery tape or soft cloth strips, tie the trunk firmly to each stake, wrapping trunk and stake in a figure-eight design.

Never use wire, nor tie the tree so tightly that the tape girdles it (cuts through the bark and underlying green cambium layer). In six months or a year, when the trunk is rock-steady in the ground, the stakes may be removed.

Larger trees need to be secured the way the mast of a sailboat is held up by its stays: Three 2-1/2– to 3-foot lengths of rebar are pounded into the ground at about 45-degree angles, equidistant from the tree, about three to four feet from the trunk. To these are attached strong wires run up to the lowermost limbs, through pieces of garden hose as collars to protect the tree's trunk, then back down to the stakes for tensioning. A variation is to use strips of woven saran webbing, available at nursery suppliers. The black webbing—flexible, adjustable, and non-chafing—comes in big rolls, and is easy to wrap from rebar to trunk to rebar again, without having to worry about running it through pieces of hose. Easy-to-use tree staking kits are also available, consisting of thick stretchy cords that secure with hooks to pins driven into the ground. Or you could build your own teepee of one-by-twos nailed to a central collar of shorter one-by-twos secured around the tree with metal banding or tie-wraps. Never nail anything directly into the trunk of a tree. *All* wounds are potential entrances for fungus.

Mulching

Mulching is recommended. It helps moderate soil temperatures, conserves water, discourages weeds, and makes a no-mow zone around the tree trunk. Keep the mulch a couple of inches away from the trunk, though, to prevent moisture buildup and rot. You might want to take advantage of the opportunity, before the tree's roots grow out of the hole, to plant some ground cover or shrubs as a floor around it. Not only will this allow the tree and its surrounding plants to develop together, but will protect the tree from one of its worst enemies: the lawnmower.

Lawnmowers and string trimmers can seriously wound a tree, cutting through the bark and the tender cambium layer that carries nutrients up from roots to tips. Once the cambium layer has been severed all the way around (girdled), the tree cannot be saved.

Even monocotyledonous trees like palms and bananas (see "Counting cotyledons," page 104) that don't have cambium layers can be laid wide open to fungus infections or invasive pests by gashes and slashes made by lawn equipment. To keep a tree healthy, keep its sheathing intact.

How to care for a young tree

Occasionally after planting, a temperamental tree will promptly drop all its leaves, frightening many novice gardeners into fits of self-accusation. Don't be taken in. Since plants lose a great deal of moisture through their leaves, shedding leaves to retain as much water as possible within its tissues is a tree's way of dealing with the shock of being planted. In fact, some landscapers purposely strip all the leaves from certain trees when planting, to avoid excessive transpiration.

So don't give up on your tree. In a few weeks—or if it's winter you may have to wait for spring—new leaves will sprout.

Over years of working with young trees, Harold has found that for the first six months of a tree's life in your garden, a weekly gallon of liquid fertilizer, diluted to half strength, will give it a nice boost for rapid growth and good root development.

There are liquid fertilizer connoisseurs who swear by Peter's 20-20-20 or Miracle-Gro or some other brand. Any of them is fine. The important thing is to actually give it, regularly, to your tree. Or you could use a special-purpose "root stimulator," available at garden centers.

After the first month, you can also begin to give the tree a monthly feeding of a handful or two (about half a cup) of a good quality balanced granular fertilizer. Sprinkle the fertilizer in a circle under the outer leaves (the drip line). As the drip line extends farther from the trunk, broaden your feeding range to extend beyond the drip line, as roots develop into the surrounding territory. After six months or so, increase the helping to a full cup of fertilizer. Feed your trees every month for the first two years, and you'll be astonished at how fast they grow—even so-called slow growers like live oaks.

After two years, you can increase the portion somewhat, and feed the tree every three months or so. The best times to feed are the end of winter, spring, summer, and fall. But there's no need to stay on a strict schedule. If you meant to feed in May, but didn't get around to it until the end of June, the tree won't hold it against you.

Shade and flowering trees will never need anything more complicated than a good quality balanced fertilizer with some minor elements—and probably not much more of that than you'd give the lawn anyway. After your citrus and other fruit trees have grown to bearing age (about two years), you might want to consider switching from their balanced diet to a special fruit-tree fertilizer formulated for greater fruit production as opposed to growth. Apply according to the package directions.

It's also often beneficial to add micro-nutrients in the form of a nutritional spray specially formulated for citrus.

Always water well the day before using dry fertilizer, and always water the fertilizer in. If you don't water the fertilizer in, grass and surrounding green tissues could be burned by contact with the fertilizer's chemicals. And anyway, the tree can't use the fertilizer until after it's dissolved and in liquid form. No matter what fertilizer you use, always follow the directions on the label.

How to train a tree

You'll know when a young tree has established itself by the exuberant way it begins to put out new leaves and branches. Your job is to determine which branches should stay and which must go.

Since a tree's leaves are the factories where fertilizer turns into food, young trees pretty much require all the leaves they can produce. So even if your tree looks a bit irregular and lumpy, it's probably best not to demand too much from it too early.

When it grows tall enough to start looking like a tree, and has a trunk diameter of at least an inch, you can gradually begin to eliminate the lateral growth—the small twigs and branches that grow from the lower part of the trunk. For the strongest, healthiest tree, Harold recommends removing these small branches very gradually, over a period of a couple of years.

If you want a tree whose lowermost branches you can walk under, as the tree grows take off more and more of the lower branches, gradually clearing the trunk to the level you like. When tiny branches pop out of the trunk, just push them off with your thumb. The

---

Going up?

Many people think the branches on a young tree will rise as the tree pushes up from the earth. They won't. Trees, like all plants, grow not from the bottom, but from the top, sending out new shoots from their branch tips. The branch you see a couple of feet from the ground will remain at that level, growing longer and thicker, for the life of the tree—or, if you're a good tree trainer, until you clip it off.

little twigs may pop out again, but if you thumb-prune a few times, eventually the tree will get the message. On some trees with relatively long branches, you might want to pinch out or snip off the terminal growth at the end of each branch to encourage further branching.

Check the tree's growth periodically—maybe the day you feed it would be convenient. Walk around the tree. Look at it from many angles. With your clippers, encourage upward growth by snipping off all the little branches that point toward the ground. When the tree starts to get dense in the middle, take out some of the crossing or rubbing interior branches. Encourage your tree into a pleasing, natural shape, with an open scaffolding of branches.

If you keep up with your tree, shaping and guiding it with pruners and loppers as it grows, its energy won't be wasted in extraneous growth. As Harold says, you can remove the branch now with a pair of clippers, or in ten years with a chain saw.

Sure-fire Shrubs

hen most people think of a shrub, they picture a bush— a naturally more or less rounded plant with a lot of stems and leaves. But is a shrub always a bush? And can other plants serve as shrubs, too? Low palm clusters, in the right setting, can serve as shrubs. Bougainvillea is a flowering woody vine, but can be shaped into a dazzlingly colorful shrub.

Even non-shrubby plants, such as crinum lilies, selloums, gingers, heliconias, and birds of paradise, can perform superbly as shrubs in a landscape design. Some trees, like seagrape and *Ficus benjamina*, can be pruned into large, bushy shrubs or even formal hedges.

Then there are the shrubs that, like good actors, can play many roles convincingly. Ligustrum (*Ligustrum recurvifolia*), a shrub with shiny, green, curvy leaves, is one of South Florida's most versatile plants. A single ligustrum responds to *laissez-faire* by becoming a good-sized natural-looking bush. Prune out the lower branches as it grows, and you'll create an interesting-looking multi-trunked tree. A row, regimentally clipped, will form a waist-high hedge—or, if you let it grow, one tall and thick enough to thwart an inquisitive neighbor with a picture window. Similarly, a flowering ixora that can turn into a 12-foot column of fire if left to its own devices is equally happy trained in the disciplines of a hedge. Orange jasmine, a classic hedge material, can be pruned into a lovely 15- to 20-foot single- or multi-trunked tree, marvelously fragrant (and often dizzy with butterflies) when it bursts into bloom several times a year. The moral of the story is: When working with shrubs, it's the function that counts.

Large shrubs are used as background plantings for lower, showier plants; shrubs make fine understory for trees; they soften the outlines of a house or the edges of a pool or pond; they round and fill the corners of an otherwise conventionally squared-off yard; some allow themselves to be sculpted into hedges. A group of the same kind of shrubs planted together, becomes a ground cover. And a big, beautiful shrub surrounded by a complementary ground cover can be a sensational specimen plant.

You won't have much trouble finding the right shrubs for your garden. In South Florida, there are shrubs in abundance, to suit every horticultural taste and landscape requirement. If you prefer flowering shrubs, gardenia, hibiscus, allamanda, oleander, crape myrtle, poinsettia, plumbago, golden dewdrop, brunfelsia, and dozens more will tempt you at the nursery. If you'd like color but not necessarily flowers, the multi-hued croton or self-descriptive copperleaf may appeal. And there are hundreds of green shrubs, with or without spotted, striped, or variegated leaves.

Playing the old standards

A standard is a shrub that has been trimmed and trained as a single-trunked tree. Some of the shrubs that lend themselves well to this treatment are *Ligustrum sinense*, orange jasmine, hibiscus, and bougainvillea.

Standard gardenias and roses (also called rose trees) are usually grafted onto straight, tall trunks, rather than trained from the ground up. As a rule, smaller standards must remain staked to stand up to the wind.

Croton

Hedging your best

In South Florida as elsewhere, hedges are used to define a property line, soften or conceal a fence (or take the place of one), or formally set off a house. Among the most formal landscape looks is the terraced hedge: two or three different kinds of hedges set one behind the other, each meticulously trimmed. At the other end of the hedge spectrum is the informal hedge, a row of identical shrubs kept in a natural shape with hand-clippers, or even allowed to grow, with a few judicious nips and snips here and there, pretty much as nature intended.

Some good green hedges

Surinam cherry (*Eugenia uniflora*). Among the most popular hedge plants in South Florida—and for good reason. Strong, fast-growing, with a dense fabric of small shiny green leaves, the Surinam cherry bears delicious pumpkin-shaped red fruit about an inch across, which attract birds. It has few, if any, insect enemies. It can be kept small and low, like boxwood, or trimmed into a living wall 12 feet tall. It's impossible to walk through a mature, healthy cherry hedge. Must be trimmed regularly to keep it looking tidy. In fact, if you don't trim a Surinam cherry plant, it will grow into a tree. Harold knows this from experience. One grew outside his bedroom window when he was a kid. He use to climb it, and he picked the cherries.

Viburnum (*Viburnum suspensum*). Classic hedge that grows to six feet tall. Tolerates some shade, but needs good irrigation. Viburnum hedges are strong, richly green, and easy to trim.

Pittosporum (*Pittosporum tobira*). The stiff-leaved, light green pittosporum, relatively slow-growing, is easy to sculpt into a strict hedge shape, or can be trimmed to a more natural look. Prefers full sun. The variegated variety is not as well suited to hedgedom.

Podocarpus (*Podocarpus macrophyllus*). Can grow into a tree 20 feet tall, but, with its flat, narrow leaves, podocarpus makes a neat, crisply cornered hedge. Looks good as the tallest in a trio of terraced hedges. Will tolerate some shade.

Arboricola (*Schefflera arboricola*). Appealing informal texture created by clusters of sunburst-shaped leaves. Good screening material. Takes well to hand-clipping in a natural shape. Left on its own, easily grows eight feet tall and higher, and can be espaliered. Cold-, shade-, and drought-tolerant.

Natal plum (*Carissa grandiflora*). Dense, waxy leaves, small white flowers, edible fruit, and impressive thorns. If you want a hedge that will keep unauthorized people and animals out, this is a good candidate. It wants to grow big and fat, but can be maintained at a reasonable size. Best pruned with hand-clippers. Gnarly interior branches make this shrub a natural for pruning into interesting bonsai shapes.

Common aralia. Fast-growing plants that grow straight up, shingling themselves with overlapping green or variegated green leaves. Excellent for fast privacy along a property line, because a mature hedge occupies hardly more than a foot of depth. Aralia also makes a handsome background for other shrubs. Aralia grows easily from cuttings. In fact, you'll probably have to grow it from cuttings, since it's almost impossible to find at nurseries. Once established, aralias are drought-resistant, but they can suffer in extreme cold.

Ficus (*Ficus benjamina*). A row of *Ficus benjaminas*—the very trees that grow into huge aerial-rooted colossi along residential roadways—can be kept under tight control with frequent trimming, to create a handsome hedge. If you don't trim them, however, they will grow into huge aerial-rooted colossi along your front walk.

Ligustrum (*Ligustrum sinense*). With its dense cloak of small green or variegated leaves, this shrub trims nicely into box shapes or other severe, formal hedging. It also makes a lovely stand-alone specimen or, in its variegated form, a fine standard. So tiny are its leaves that you might be tempted to try topiary, but things grow so quickly here that trimming would become your life's work.

Some flowering hedges

Ixora. The newer varieties in nurseries today are real improvements on the older ones, with big showy flowers on strong plants. Very popular are the Maui (orange) and Nora Grant (pink) ixoras. You can clip ixora into traditional strict, formal shapes (though severe shaping inhibits flowering), or shape them gently for a well-groomed natural look. Ixora "Super King," wants to grow too big for a hedge, but makes a gorgeous specimen plant.

Bougainvillea (*Bougainvillea spectabilis*). Not usually considered good hedge material because pruning discourages blooming,

How to make an aralia hedge

To start with, you need enough sturdy cuttings of equal length, 18 to 36 inches long, to plant six to eight inches apart. To obtain your cuttings, do a deal with a friend or neighbor: aralia cuttings in exchange for help trimming their hedge.

Poke holes in the ground with a digging bar, and bury at least four inches of stem. Tie the cuttings to a fence, or stake for support if needed. Trim off the tops evenly, and water thoroughly. Don't worry if all the leaves fall off.

Water every day for two weeks, then taper off. After new leaves appear, begin a program of regular trimming, including, when the aralia is thick and healthy, periodically pruning some stalks very short so they will sprout closer to the base of the plant. A row of fishtail ferns across the bottom helps hide the aralea's knobby knees.

and blooming is one of a bougainvillea's major missions and most powerful attractions (*spectabilis* means "visually striking"). The exception is the purple variety, which, if kept on a rigorous clipping schedule, makes an elegant formal hedge of dense green foliage interspersed with brilliant color (it will also twine high into trees, if this is the effect you're after). The relatively new dwarf variety, with bold magenta flowers, a horizontal habit, and a profile just a couple of feet high, can make an attractive low naturally-shaped hedge. Bougainvilleas are very thorny—most of them are, anyway—which can also be an advantage in a hedge. They do best in full sun.

Oleander (*Nerium oleander*). Thick with ribbony leaves, fragrant oleander, especially the new lower-growing varieties, makes a good naturally shaped hedge. It isn't fussy about soils, and is salt-tolerant. The news isn't all good, however. Oleander sap is poisonous, something to keep in mind when you're looking for long, straight canes for toasting marshmallows. Also, oleanders have their very own caterpillar—the black-furred orange oleander caterpillar—so if you don't like to see gobbled leaves, be prepared for continual warfare. Before you reach for the sprayer, however, you should know that oleander caterpillars metamorphose into striking red, white, and blue Uncle Sam moths.

Hibiscus. Beautiful hedge plants, though after seven or ten years, they tend to get woody and may need to be replaced. Best varieties for hedges are Painted Lady, also called Miami Lady (watermelon pink), and common red. A row of tall, arching La France, with its gracefully cascading pink blooms, make a graceful unclipped hedge. Less successful are the fancy grafted hybrids; these are best used as specimen plants.

Orange jasmine (*Murraya paniculata*).
Densely covered with tiny leaves, and bears fragrant white blossoms. Can grow to 20 feet, but takes nicely to trimming. Doesn't mind sandy soil.

Secrets of a happy hedge

Close, but not too close. Hedge plants should be planted close enough together to mesh into a seamless unit, but not so close that they strangle each other. For most plants, about 18 inches from center to center is about right.

Leave room for the hedge to grow, which means not too close to a fence, building, or sidewalk. If you leave plenty of room on the other side of a hedge, you'll be able to walk behind it to trim or work.

A hedge will not hesitate to grow through a chain-link fence—an advantage if you want your fence camouflaged. But if the fence borders a neighbor's yard, you'll need to walk on their property to trim the other side. If you're unsure how they feel about this, better leave yourself a pathway between hedge and fence.

Clip, clip, clip. A hedge is a partnership between you and nature. Nature creates the plant; you create the hedge. So do your part, and start trimming early.

Every time the plant puts on six inches of growth, swallow hard and trim off three inches. This is the only way to ensure the plant will grow bushy as it grows up. If you wait for the hedge to get tall before you trim, you'll either wind up with a leggy hedge with all its new growth at the top, or have to cut off a lot of hard-won growth later on to encourage lower bushiness.

Try to trim the sides of the hedge straight up and down, or, better yet, with a barely discernible slope inward toward the top. This lets the bottom of the hedge get good light, so the leaves will stay green and thick all the way to the ground.

Alternate style: the natural look. Less formal hedges can be trimmed with a hand clipper; you shape them just enough to keep them looking neat. This is an especially good method for flowering hedges, since it lets you preserve the flower clusters.

Pinch an inch

Whenever you want a plant to grow thick and bushy, frequently pinch off all the small tips of new growth rather than cutting large pieces of stem.

Shrubs in the landscape

A frame for the house

Virtually any house looks more inviting when set off by a planted frame. But the frame doesn't have to crowd the picture. It can be too dark for some plants way back under the eaves, and they really aren't happy crammed against the wall. When the bad news comes that your house needs to be tented for termites, unless there's room for caring workers to maneuver the tent fabric behind the shrubs, anything planted snug against the house will die with the bugs. It makes much more sense to begin your planting areas beyond the roof overhang, where the shrubs will get more light, and you'll be able to walk and work in the space behind them (which can be covered with mulch or pebbles, and will soon become invisible behind the greenery).

Which shrubs to choose?

Selecting shrubs to be used together and placing them so they complement one another are part of the art of South Florida gardening. The secret is knowing how to combine the

abundantly available
forms and textures into
a pleasing whole. There
are various ways to do
this. One is the variations-
on-a-theme approach in
which all the plants have
the same basic texture,
in different forms: all
long, narrow leaves of different
sizes, densities, and shades of green,
for instance, or a harmonious
blending of rounded and heart-
shaped leaves. Or you could mix
contrasting leaf forms in a sort
of English border approach.

Spider lily

A mistake common to novices
is to buy one of every kind of plant
and arrange them in a mixed bed.
Much better to get several of each
kind and let one group drift into the
next. And unless you're making a hedge,
shrubs usually look best massed in groups
rather than planted single file.

Monstera
deliciosa

When you get to thinking about the form
and textures of plants, choosing specific ones
becomes easier, because you are able to narrow the field to the plants that fit your needs.

If you prefer the long, ribbony, or spiky-
looking leaves, you'll head for the bamboo
palms, crinum and spider lilies, corn plants
or other dracaenas, walking iris, liriopes.

For a grouping of more rounded textures,
you'll pick out the jungly looking *Monstera
deliciosa* with their Swiss-cheese leaves, spade-
leafed alocasias, *Pittosporum wheelerii*, and
the naturally rounded *Ilex vomitoria*, a holly
whose leaves practitioners of folk medicine
once boiled to produce a potion to do just what
its name implies.

Even when you're considering a flowering shrub for a mixed planting, its form and texture when not in flower should be a primary consideration.

Gardenias, euphorbias, crape myrtles, gingers and heliconias, birds of paradise, and hibiscus can look marvelous in your mosaic of shrubs, even when not in bloom. The flowers are a beautiful bonus.

The choice of shrubs is further slimmed according to the conditions (sunny, shady, moist, dry) in which they'll make their home.

Covering ground

As a ground cover, grass has one big advantage. It can be walked on. However, if you want to do less of the mowing and other maintenance grass requires, if you have rocky, steep, or shaded areas where grass won't readily grow, if you want to stop the grass short of a tree, or if you would like to unify your planting areas and set them off from the lawn, there are other attractive ways to cover the ground. Whether you use nonliving ground covers like pebbles and mulches, or cover the ground with plants, the objective is the same. Ground covers make the place look nicer. A shade tree growing in the lawn can be visually linked to a nearby grouping of shrubbery by a curving swath of pine-bark mulch or by a carpet of ferns or bromeliads or spathiphyllums or other plants. The wise use of ground covers is good landscape technique. Which ground cover to use is a matter of conditions, vision, and taste.

Of bark and rock

Some commonly used non-plant ground covers are pea rock (limestone broken into pea-sized bits), red river rock (also known as Chattahoochee), marble chips or other rock, and pine bark and similar organic mulches. These ground covers frame and define thickly planted areas, and are useful where it's impractical to use plants or grass, such as the floor of a shade house or your dog's outdoor run. Pebbles and mulch don't usually replace grass altogether, but Harold recalls one yard in South Florida whose "lawn" was completely paved in Chattahoochee, and centered with a gilded lawnmower mounted as sculpture.

Things to know about using nonliving ground covers:

• Stone and mulches shouldn't touch the plants themselves. Air must circulate at the bases of trees and shrubs to prevent rot.

• Sometimes mulch can harbor bugs and other wildlife.

• When organic mulches break down, they can rob nearby plants of nitrogen (the remedy for this is a bit more nitrogen in the fertilizer or an extra shot of nitrogen separately).

• Stones and pebbles are not a good idea for a path you intend to trim with a power edger. They can nick a blade or be launched like missiles.

• Some lightweight mulches can float away in a heavy rain if not hemmed in by a curb or edging.

Ground covers that grow

Any shrub, even industrial strength ones like philodendron selloums, which typically spread six feet in all directions, can be used as ground cover. Some, however, are especially well suited:

Bromeliads. Some varieties thrive when massed on the ground in sun or dappled shade. If you don't want them catching every leaf and flower that falls from above, you might limit them to use around palms that don't drop a lot of debris.

Mosquito non grata

If you're concerned that mosquitoes may be breeding in your bromeliads, you can foil them. Add a few drops of vegetable or Volck oil to each cup, or sprinkle a light dusting of Sevin, or just do as Harold does: Flush the varmints out with a garden hose.

Also, it's wise to do some research before selecting bromeliads, since some won't bloom without sufficient sun, and others won't tolerate shade.

Selloum (*Philodendron selloum*). A jungly-looking plant with huge dark green leaves. Especially good under trees like avocado or sea grape, to filter and hide the tree's big leaves as they fall.

Ferns. Excellent for the shady area around a tree, where leaves can filter through. Because they have relatively shallow roots, you can plant them within a few feet of even a mature tree without disturbing the tree's roots. When they expand beyond the boundaries you've set, just pull out the extras and use them to start another ferny area somewhere else.

Blue Daze (*Evolvulus glomeratus*). Low-growing, with silvery green leaves and small bright blue flowers. Can wilt in extreme droughts, but fairly drought-tolerant which makes it good for planters. Does fine in sun or partial shade, and makes a lovely border. It does better if trimmed back from time to time. Harold gave Blue Daze its popular common name.

Mondo grass (*Ophiopogon japonicus*) or lily turf. If you like the look of grass, but don't want to mow around your shrubs, mondo grass, either the regular (one-foot) variety or the stubby miniature, is totally grasslike. It's low, narrow-leaved, and will spread until you call a halt. Excellent for places where grass dies out, like shady areas under trees, or on hard-to-mow slopes.

Liriope. The three-foot-tall Ever-green Giant variety, and the 18-inch green or green-and-white variegated (*Liriope muscari*), make excellent dense grassy borders and ground covers.

Society garlic (*Tulbaghia violacea*). Grassy clumps of foliage with clusters of tiny lavender flowers. Likes full sun and soil on the sandy side. Makes an effective border.

Spider plant (*Chlorophytum comosum*). The popular hanging-basket plant grows in nature on the ground, where it propagates by tossing its tethered plantlets to take root nearby. The process covers a lot of ground surprisingly quickly. You can help things along by spacing the plantlets closely, to make a nice dense cover.

Sprengeri (*Asparagus densaflorus*). Often called Sprengeri fern, though it's really a member of the lily family, this plant is low-growing, with long arching stems of delicate light green lacework that look lovely cascading over a bordering curb or a planter. Tiny white flowers are followed by pea-sized fruit that ripens bright red.

Sprengeri is also thick, thorny, and practically indestructible, impervious to virtually everything, including the weed killers Round-up and Kleenup (an advantage if you want to get rid of grass that has grown into it; even so, to be on the safe side, Harold recommends not taking this practice to extremes).

Cuphea (*Cuphea hyssopifolia*) or Mexican heather. A stocky little bush dotted with magenta or white starlike flowers. Makes a nice swath among taller shrubs. Needs good irrigation.

Walking iris (*Trimezia martinicensis*). A graceful plant with irisy leaves and small yellow flowers that look very much like miniature irises. Grows in spreading clumps three feet tall. Likes sun or light shade, and tolerates dry and windy conditions.

Pilea (*Pilea microphylla*). Pea green or the newer, darker green variety, pilea or artillery fern spreads nicely and has an interesting bubbly texture. Does well in sun, shade, cold, and drought, and propagates easily from cuttings. The bad news is that it's a favorite dish for snails, so keep the bait handy.

Lantana. Spreads a carpet of color in sunny areas. The dwarf gold variety, *Lantana camara,* is best; it's native to the coasts of South Florida. Also good is the lilac-flowered *L. montevidenis*. Other varieties tend to grow too big to control.

Day lily (*Hemerocallis*). Spiky green leaves and bright yellow flowers that look spectacular massed in full sun. Use only the varieties that do well in the tropics. A favorite is Aztec Gold.

Pothos (*Epipremnum aureum*). Cousin to the common and ubiquitous trailing household philodendron, pothos becomes a surprisingly solid and attractive ground cover when planted in shady areas. Inexpensive, too, because it roots so easily from cuttings. But beware. If it encounters a tree or wall, it climbs, generating monster leaves up to two feet long, and takes on a new name: **Hunter's robe.** Many gardeners love this effect. If you don't, you'll need to keep your pothos on a short leash.

Anthuriums and spathiphyllums. These tropical-looking plants cover ground quite elegantly, by creating mounds of graceful greenery surmounted by spathes held high in areas ranging from light to dappled and even deeper shade.

Coontie (*Zamia pumila*). A native plant with a palmish look that grows in clusters of long compound leaves about 18 inches tall.

Wedelia (*Wedelia trilobata*). A common dark-leafed creeper with bright yellow flowers that can cover a lot of ground fast. Salt-tolerant and popular near the shore, it's especially good in areas bounded by concrete curbs or walks (and can become quite aggressive if not contained in this way). If it gets too feisty, just mow it down. In a couple of weeks it'll be back smiling. A word of caution: Once wedelia gets into a lawn, it becomes "weed-elia," and unless you don't mind yellow flowers popping up in your grass, you'll need to get out the weed killer.

Making it in the shade

If you have trees, you have shade—and an opportunity to become acquainted with a whole new realm of gardening, since most of South Florida's shade-loving plants are descended from the tropical rainforest. These plants grow not in darkness, but in filtered light, in still, humid air, and in moist (not wet) soil. Their natural habitat is warm, so they are not always cold-tolerant (though if they fail in a freeze, most will come back).

For your shady places, look to the aroid family: alocasias, dracaenas, dieffenbachias, selloums, anthuriums, caladiums, and *Monstera deliciosa*. Try also ferns, ivies, pepperomias, mondo grass, and pothos. Many shade-loving plants are so fond of low light conditions that they'll move happily indoors with you.

Anthurium

Some good choices include bird's nest ferns, with their 30-inch fronds in a nestlike rosette; Kentia or bamboo palms; and the curly Ming aralia and elegant false aralia.

Shade-loving plants generally run the spectrum of greens, with many variegations (such as the silver-streaked or gold-spattered leaves of the aglaonemas), but there are shade-loving plants that flower, too. The one you see most in South Florida is impatiens, low-growing, vivacious bloomers that create delightful splashes of color in a cool garden glade. Others are anthuriums, with waxy-looking flowers in red, pink, white and green; the white spathiphyllum or peace lily; shade-loving gingers and heliconias in show-stopping shapes and colors; orchids; many bromeliads; and the shrimp plant, three-to-five-feet tall, and topped with yellow or salmon-colored flowers so like their name you may be tempted to dip them in cocktail sauce.

A vine romance

Vines can look spectacular or set a romantic mood, cascading over a wall, clinging to a fence, even rambling overhead. Consider a pathway covered with an arcade of vines or a gazebo laced with viny fragrance. For a patio roof, how about flowers? Just stretch chicken wire across corner posts and plant a vine at each post.

There are two kinds of vines: woody, which must be tied to or woven through their supports, and twining, which cling by themselves. All vines grow upward, and tend to lose foliage at their bases. That's why you see most of the activity at the top. Don't be disheartened. As the vine continues to grow, the leaves and flowers will cascade down again.

Some favorite woody vines:

Mandevilla. Charming nonstop trumpet-shaped flowers in bright pink or yellow. But a favorite dish of caterpillars.

Stephanotis (*Stephanotis floribunda*). Also called bridal bouquet and Madagascar jasmine. Bears glamorous clusters of richly fragrant white blossoms. Roots should be shaded, but vine does best in dappled sun.

Allamanda. The yellow-flowering *against fence* brown-bud allamanda is the vining variety (dramatic affixed to a redwood fence). Flowers on new growth, so don't be too quick to prune.

Bleeding heart vine (*Clerodendrum thomsoniae*). Red and white or red and pink flowers that may put you in mind of fuschias.

Petrea or Queen's wreath (*Petrea volubilis*). The wisteria of the South. Has sandpapery leaves and is covered with racemes of delicate blue-violet or white flowers in spring.

Bougainvillea. Probably the most famous subtropical vine in the world. It comes in scores of dazzling colors. When its growth is young and succulent, it can be tied to or woven through chain link. Trained in this way, a single plant can cover 50 feet of fence. Or train a pair of bougainvilleas, in companionable colors, up the side of a porch or carport. Trim off any small branch that breaks out along the trunk to create a interesting bare stalk with a crown of lavishly blooming arching sprays. Once the vines are established, you needn't bother feeding or watering too much. Mature bougainvilleas seem to thrive on what Harold calls "benign neglect."

Some favorite twining vines:

Flame vine (*Pyrostegia ignea*). Cheerful clusters of tubular orange flowers whose fiery color is intensified by planting in full sun.

Garlic vine (*Cydista aequinoctialis*). Can turn an ordinary fence into a thing of beauty, with its big showy clusters of lavender flowers. Up close, its foliage has a distinct garlic scent.

Pandora vine. Beautiful big bell-shaped powder-pink flowers that look magnificent cascading down a wall or hanging overhead.

Confederate jasmine (*Trachelospermum jasminoides*) has white flowers and can grow to 20 feet high if supported; **Carolina jasmine (*Gelsemium sempervirens*)** has bright yellow blooms, and is poisonous.

against front porch Red

Passion flower vine (*Passiflora edulis*). Exotic silky-looking blooms. The purple-flowered variety seems to do better than the red. If you like butterflies, plant this vine. Caterpillars will chew leaves, but the butterflies will be worth it.

***Ficus repens* or *pumila*.** Affectionately known in Dade County as the Metro-Rail vine because it covers many of the elevated railroad's concrete supports, *Ficus repens* has tiny leaves and tenacious hold-fasts that cling to concrete and wood.

against wooden fence

If you like the look of ivy-covered cottages, this vine is for you. It's a true ficus, though. If you don't trim it, at the top of your wall it will turn into a tree, complete with aerial roots. It will even bear figs!

Thunbergia (*Thunbergia grandiflora*). A glorious vine with heart-shaped leaves and cascading tumbles of blue flowers. The variety *alba* has white flowers.

A kick of color

In the subtropical landscape, the tropical leaves (and in some cases even the stems and trunks of plants and trees) might give your garden all the color it needs. Besides the expected salad of greens, foliage turns up all snazzed up in reds, yellows, grays, pinks, purples, and variegations in tiger stripes, leopard spots, borders, splotches, and speckles of virtually every combination.

Ti plant

If subtle splashes of foliar color are what you're after, crotons, lilies, gingers, cordylines (ti plants), dracaenas, acalphas, bananas, bromeliads, and caladiums—just for starters — are worth investigating. For those who want more exclamatory color, or who love flowers among the foliage, subtropical plants will accommodate you in several different ways.

Bulbs, corms, and tubers

Some northern bulbs—tulips, hyacinths, daffodils, paperwhites, irises, crocuses, and the like—can be forced in South Florida for indoor bloom, just like anywhere else. But outdoors, these bulbs just won't light.

South Florida's flower bulbs and tubers tend to produce more jungly, exotic-looking flowers like amaryllis, crinum lily, gloriosa lily, canna lily, and gorgeous heliconias. You can come pretty close to the idea of a northern daffodil with our Eucharist lily, and the dainty rain lily resembles and behaves somewhat like a crocus.

Perennials

Perennials in South Florida are long-term shrubs, ground covers, and flowers, most of which bloom all year.

Perennial flowers include pentas, walk-

Periwinkle

Impatiens

ing iris, society garlic, rock roses, purslane, and periwinkle. Some northern perennials, such as geraniums, chrysanthemums, and impatiens, are treated as annuals in South Florida.

Annuals

During the cooler months, almost any annual will grow in South Florida, making a nice splash of color against an all-green background, or filling in for a cycling bulb or perennial in a flower border.

Since the whole point of annual flowers is color, and since they are by nature temporary, you can feel free to indulge your experimental impulses. It's fun to try different kinds and combinations each season. Keep the neighbors guessing.

Annual flowers are very useful in the landscape. You can plant a whole bright swath, or tuck a few here and there. And annuals are attractive and inexpensive space fillers while you're waiting for new shrubs to grow up.

Because annuals live their whole lives in a relatively brief blaze, most require full sun, plenty of water, and regular fertilizing to live up to their colorful potential. The exception is impatiens, the most popular annual, which usually prefers filtered light.

During fall, winter, and spring, you'll find benches loaded with annuals at garden centers all over South Florida. A few stalwarts can even brave South Florida summers, notably marigolds, zinnias, salvias, and celosias.

How to get it right the first time

So large are the number and variety of shrubs that will thrive in South Florida gardens that when you start making choices it's not uncommon to feel confused or even somewhat overwhelmed. To select wisely, the smart thing is to do a lot of looking, asking, and reading.

Drive around attractive neighborhoods for inspiration and ideas. Harold does. If something arrests his attention, he walks up and knocks on the door. Really. Most gardeners are delighted to chat about their plants, and will be happy to give you the benefit of their experience, as well as, sometimes, a cutting or seed.

Don't be satisfied with planting what everyone else has. Be aware that, for instance, *ixora* implies lots of different varieties. *Clerodendrum* encompasses not just the common bleeding heart vine, but several other shrubs and vines. The same is true of crinum lilies, aroids, euphorbias, and hundreds of other tropical and subtropical plant groups. So take time to look around. You might come up with a treasure.

It can be especially rewarding to visit specialist landscape nurseries in your quest to find and learn about unusual plants. The people who run these nurseries are usually old South Florida hands, and can give you expert advice

A fling with seeds

Though starter plants are the quickest route to annual color, some South Florida gardeners have excellent luck with seeds.

A neighbor of Harold's, tired of seeing the naked earth where cars habitually cut the corner of his grass swale, hoed up the ground along the road and tossed in some zinnia seeds. The ensuing mixed chorus of cheerful faces had the whole block smiling, and kept all those cars off, too.

Lots of plants besides annuals can be grown from seed, as well. Some that are pariculary interesting are flowering trees, gingers and heliconias, palms, and many shrubs and vines.

Ask a neighbor for a few seeds from an attractive plant, or look for unusual seeds for sale at events held at nearby South Florida botanical gardens.

based on their personal experience. For instance:

• Plants have individual characteristics and preferences. If your shrub wants sun, give it sun. If it needs lots of water, don't plant it with shrubs that like things on the dry side.

• Choose good quality plants. Everyone likes a bargain, but keep value in mind. You can't expect stellar performance from a spindly, second-rate plant.

• Know how big each plant is going to get, and give it room to grow. Some gardeners like the overlapped and interwoven look of planting things somewhat closer than recommended, but too close risks scrawny, unhealthy plants, and almost guarantees a lot of future pruning.

• Plant plants properly, and take care of them. They're part of the family now.

Grass with Class

n most civilized neighborhoods, a lawn is *de rigueur*. A well-kept lawn sets off your plants to advantage and comes in handy as a place for people to sit while they admire your garden. Unless you live on the beach, or in the Keys, or in a place like Coconut Grove (where you can barely see the houses for the shrubbery and trees) you will probably want a lawn.

The way your lawn looks bears directly on the appearance of your property. You might spend thousands on trees and rare plants, but if your lawn is shabby, your yard will look terrible. On the other hand, you may have a grand total of six shrubs in an advanced case of weeds, but if your lawn is magnificent, people will say you've got the knack.

How big a lawn you want is another question entirely, and no trifling consideration since your investment of time, effort, and money varies largely with size. But having a nice lawn doesn't mean you have to obsess over it. Some people turn their grass into a hobby, spending weekends crawling around pulling up every little weed. Harold's philosophy is somewhat more casual. "If it's green," he says, "mow it."

But even with allowable imperfections, a

decent lawn requires a certain commitment: frequent mowing and trimming, regular irrigation and fertilizing, and pest control as required. Ergo, if you want to reduce your commitment, and don't wish to hire the job out, the only alternative is to reduce the size of your lawn. You do this by replacing areas of grass with trees, shrubs, and mulch. Over the long haul, plants and mulch are far less cash-, water-, and labor-intensive than grass.

This is not to suggest you delete the grass entirely. A nice lawn can be an important part of family life, including providing a place for the volleyball net and areas where the children can safely play. And well-tended lawn areas are an undeniably attractive foil for your garden plants.

Lawn shrinking doesn't need to be accomplished all at once. First you take out just enough to plant the islands of trees and shrubs on your garden plan. As the canopies of the trees and girth of the shrubs expand, the lawn gradually recedes. Eventually, you might want to remove additional grass to unite neighboring planted areas into one natural sweep. After a few years of this, you can reduce your lawn by a third or even half, just by attrition, while creating a leafy landscape set off by small, neat, satisfyingly controllable areas of healthy green and attractive grass.

The grass menagerie

Unless your house is brand new, you probably already have a lawn. Most likely it's a lawn of the most popular grass in Florida (note to transplanted Northerners: No, it's not crabgrass)—St. Augustine grass.

Northern grasses do about as well as polar bears in South Florida's heat and humidity. Some people obstinately insist on trying them anyway. Other subtropical grasses sound appealing, so people try those. Eventually, for one reason or another, most of them give up and go back to St. Augustine. This doesn't mean for sure that St. Augustine grass will be best for you, however. So before you decide, meet the rest of the field:

Centipede grass

If you live in Dade County's Redland area, where a great deal of farming is done, centipede grass could be a good choice. Although centipede grass may not be as pretty as well-maintained St. Augustine (it looks like a miniature version, and is known locally as the "poor man's lawn,") it has attractive advantages. Chinch bugs dislike it, and it requires hardly any mowing. All it wants is some water and a bit of fertilizer once in a while, including a periodic dose of iron to keep it a good green. If a bare spot develops, you can toss in some seeds to fill in.

Centipede grass is a creeper with tremendous resolve. Back when the University of Miami was being built, the grounds surrounding the new buildings were nothing but rock and rubble punctuated by scrubby pines and palmettos. Someone planted some centipede grass, which quickly engulfed everything in its path, knocking out the weeds as it advanced. You've got to have respect for a grass like that. If you don't enjoy mowing, you've got to love it.

Sow smart

If you mix grass seed with an equal part of Milorganite, the seed will be more evenly distributed, and have something to eat when it sprouts.

Bermuda grass

Lots of golfers wish their lawns could be as beautiful as a putting green. It can. Florida putting-green grass is Bermuda grass. Bermuda grass is gorgeous. It is also, without even a close competitor, the highest-maintenance lawn grass in Florida. The common variety can be grown from seed, but the improved ones are usually purchased as sod. Either way, only an expensive reel-type mower will properly cut it, weeds love it, and families of fungi have reunions in it. If you dedicate your life to it (as golf course maintenance crews do), you will have the most beautiful lawn on the block. Most people give up after a while, and put in St. Augustine.

Zoysia grass

Zoysia is found in quite a few South Florida lawns. It arouses extreme reactions in people. At the nursery sales counter, one person will demand zoysia sod, even if he has to wait an extra week and pay double for it, and the person behind him in line will detest zoysia and want to know how to get rid of it.

Zoysia is small-bladed, naturally light green, and extremely tough. It grows slowly but aggressively, and somewhat humpily, so a zoysia lawn is rarely perfectly flat. Zoysia loves to sink its long roots into your flower beds (your lawn edger is no help here), and will tunnel under a four-foot-wide sidewalk to assault the grass on the other side. If it invades a St. Augustine lawn, send in reinforcements or the zoysia will eventually win.

In the past, every few years zoysia lawn owners would set one edge of their lawn on fire, and it would do a slow, smoldering burn toward the other edge, controlled from behind with a garden hose. This violent procedure, far from the act of a crazed zoysia hater bent on destroying his grass, was used to burn out thatch and encourage new green growth. Six weeks later, the charred yard would be transformed into a fresh, beautiful lawn. Do not try this yourself; the law now forbids the practice.

Zoysia is The Grass that Won't Die—unless, of course, you want it to live. Fungus loves it; there's hardly a zoysia lawn in South Florida without at least one brown dead patch. Zoysia should be cut with a reel-type mower, because a rotary mower will tug and scalp it, laying it wide open to fungus. However, if well looked after, zoysia can make a beautiful velvety lawn, and it works especially well in a very small lawn you can easily keep an eye on. Because it grows so slowly, Zoysia is a good choice for the spaces between stepping stones or the broken stones of a patio. When it starts inching over the stones you can just whack it back into line with a hatchet.

Bahia grass

Bahia grasses are pasture grasses, and they're just fine—in pastures. Bahia is also used in highway median strips and beside the shoulders of roads. You've probably noticed how this works: Workmen lay sod and abandon it. The grass grows three feet tall and looks dreadful. Finally someone mows—and leaves all the cuttings, making an absolute mess. Don't write your state representative. It's all done on purpose. First the bahia is allowed to grow until its seeds set. Stalks are left after mowing so the seeds that fall into the earth will be shaded by the chaff while they germinate. The grass comes up lush and healthy, after which it's regularly maintained. At least that's the plan. If it doesn't happen, *then* write your state representative.

Bahia grass is frequently used on sandy soils where its long roots can penetrate to the subterranean moisture. Take a ride along Skyline Drive in Jensen Beach, and you'll see long stretches of bahia growing in the sand. In dry season, if nobody waters it, bahia will get so brown you'd swear it was dead. But give it one rain and it turns green again. While Bahia grass looks OK as you're riding by at 40 miles per hour, as soon as you stop and take a look at it, you can see there's quite a bit of earth among the blades. That's why you don't see it in many lawns.

St. Augustine grass

St. Augustine is the umbrella name for several strains and hybrids of grass. The first widely used strain was called Rose Lawn. Then came Bitter Blue, a great favorite for many years, though it was highly susceptible to chinch bugs, which can suck grass brown. Floratam, which appeared on the market in the early 80s and quickly became South Florida's most popular lawn grass, was at first chinch-bug resistant, reducing this nemesis for years. Gradually, however, the critters started developing a taste for it. Researchers are constantly working on new hybrids of St. Augustine grass, trying to come up with one variety that will be drought-resistant, grows well in shade, and will turn a chinch bug's stomach. A new no-mow hybrid is also being worked on.

St. Augustine grass has an attractive deep blue-green color, thick growing habit, and comparatively low maintenance. It's also the most accessible lawn grass in South Florida, sold as sod at virtually any well-stocked neighborhood garden center.

In the old days, sod didn't come in the handy rectangles you can tile like pieces of carpeting to form an instant lawn. You'd spot-sod, planting four- or six-inch squares of St. Augustine a foot apart, and, since it was rainy season (you'd never start a lawn any other time) the grass would gradually spread to fill the bald spots in between. Or you'd buy a bag of stolons—the arching runners that make new grass plants—and start your lawn with those. You can still use plugs or stolons, but modern sod is a lot easier.

St. Augustine isn't perfect. It can be attacked by chinch bugs, army worms, and fungus, and it does get weeds. Weeds, however, are usually a sign of improper maintenance.

Lawns need three things: water, fertilizer, and regular mowing. If you neglect any one of them, your lawn will begin to pale and thin. Nature abhors a vacuum. If she spots a bare patch, she will put in something green. And, as you've probably noticed, she likes to surprise you.

> **Well-tailored sod**
>
> Sod should be fitted so no gullies show in between tiles. Water daily until you can tug on a handful without yanking it loose (about two or three weeks).

A lawn story

Chapter 1: Water

Grass should be watered deeply and thoroughly, to encourage its roots to dig down as far as possible. If you sprinkle lightly and frequently, the water—and the roots that absorb it—will stay near the surface. For the greenest lawn, when the weather is dry, give it an inch of water. You can measure with a rain gauge or an ordinary cake pan three times a week in rocky or sandy soils, when needed if you live on water-retaining marl. Harold, who gardens on marl, has run his sprinklers a total of four times in ten years. Your grass will develop long healthy roots, helping it do better during droughts when watering is restricted.

If you wish to conserve water, pay attention to your lawn. Grass is a good communicator. It will tell you when it needs to be watered. Wilted blades fold in half, exposing their undersides and giving the lawn a grayish appearance. Wilted grass does not readily spring back after being driven across or walked on, so you'll see tire tracks or footprints on your lawn. This slight wilt is caused by reduced turgor, or water pressure, within the cells. Experts recommend deep watering when about a third of the lawn shows signs of slight wilt. Waiting until the grass blades curl is waiting too long; the plant could be damaged through lack of water. However, if the leaves of grass are lying nice and flat, they're already turgid or full of water, and any additional water applied will be water wasted.

Chapter 2: Fertilize

Two or three times a year, South Florida lawns need to be fertilized. Harold has found that an excellent fertilizer is Milorganite, Milwaukee's famous recycled sewage sludge, or Florida Organix, Dade County's version, if you can find it. Other counties may also recycle waste into garden fertilizers. It's a good idea to use them if they're available. Both are long-lasting, and, because they are organic, won't burn your grass even if you don't water it in right away. You can also use a general-purpose balanced fertilizer, or, if you wish, a high-nitrogen lawn fertilizer. These usually contain relatively quick-release nitrogen, and may

require more frequent applications. All fertilizers should be applied according to package
directions.

Chapter 3: Mow

St. Augustine grass does not look good in
a crew cut. It should be kept at least two or
three inches long. Other kinds of grasses may
be cut a bit lower. Bermuda and Zoysia grasses
may be kept quite short. Still, in summer, most
grasses appreciate being permitted to grow
somewhat taller than in the cooler months. The
grass's blades are its leaves, which not only
produce food for the plant, but also shade its
rhizomes—the horizontal stems that run at
or just below ground level. Cut the grass too
short and the sun will burn the rhizomes, giving your grass a nice tan.

Because St. Augustine is a robust grower,
ideally it should be mowed at least weekly in
summer. In very rainy periods it might really
need a trim even more often than that. It's a
good idea not to let grass grow too high between mowings. Grass looks best, grows best,
thickens best, and discourages weeds best
when not too much of the blade tips is sliced
off at once.

Occasionally the grass is going to get
ahead of you. It happens to everyone. You go
on vacation, or it rains for two weeks straight,
and by the time you're finally able to confront
the lawn with your mower—Yikes!—it's monster grass. The temptation is to cut it quickly
back to size, but you really shouldn't. Having
grown used to the shade of its long blades,
the rhizomes are very likely to burn
if suddenly exposed. Better to
shorten the grass gradually
over three or four mowings.
You can do this by raising
the blade for the first cut, and

lowering it incrementally over the next few mowings until the proper grass height is achieved.

Your mower blade must be sharp. Dull blades invite fungus. If your grass looks as if it has been torn off rather than cleanly cut, it is time to have the mower's blade sharpened.

The clippings controversy

Some people say leaving grass clippings on the lawn is bad because it looks untidy. But if you don't relish lugging bags of clippings to the dump or the compost heap, you might be clever enough to do as Harold does: Mow in such a way that the clippings are cast where they can be re-mowed on the next few passes. This chops them small enough to filter back through the grass.

Even if you're a neatnik who carefully rakes and disposes of clippings, you might not be doing the grass much good. As in all plants, the leaf-tips contain stored nutrients the grass plants need. Take them away, and you'll have to replenish these nutrients with more frequent fertilization.

The new generation of mulching lawnmowers resolves the question nicely whether you're an expert mower or not. They simply chew up the clippings into tiny specks and spit them right straight down to the grass roots. This saves on fertilizer as well as landfill space, since the mulched clippings recycle all their valuable nutrients back down into the soil.

To keep a lawn looking neat, the finishing touches are edging and trimming. Some people do both every time they mow; their lawns look perfectly manicured all the time. Others edge every other mowing or even less frequently, just to keep the grass from growing over the sidewalk and into the shrubbery. Be advised, though, that the more often you edge, the easier it is to do.

Grass-roots campaigns

Sooner or later, you'll be called upon to fight the good fight against those who would have your lawn (or you) for dinner.

To kill insects of all kinds (including chinch bugs, army worms, grubs, fleas, ticks, fire ants, or whatever else is bugging you), you could spray liquid chemical through a hose-end sprayer. Harold finds it much easier and more positive to broadcast the chemical in granular form.

Fungus is a different story.

Lawn fungus can be frustrating. Sometimes it will go away if you ignore it. Sometimes it will surrender to one spray of fungicide. But other times you can spray for six weeks running and still lose the war. Fungus has been known (rarely, thank goodness) to massacre entire lawns. You just have to do your best, and hope. If the fungus wins, you still have a last resort. You can buy some sod and start over.

How to diagnose a lawn problem

When to suspect chinch bugs:

• Chinch bugs love St. Augustine grass. If almost all the St. Augustine grass in the affected area is yellow, brown, or dead—but the weeds and other kinds of grass in the brown area are still green—suspect chinch bugs.

• If you had chinch bugs in the same place last year, there's a good chance they're at it again. They can be controlled, but, as with any insect pest, seldom completely eliminated.

• Chinch bugs enjoy the residual heat of concrete or asphalt, so be suspicious if the brown area is near a walk or driveway.

• Chinch bug damage shows up more quickly as rain or irrigation decreases. This is because the chinch bugs continue lapping up what they feel is their share, but in dry weather the moisture isn't replaced.

To control chinch bugs, use Dursban or Diazinon in a drench or crystals, making sure the chemical solution penetrates down through grass roots and soil. Chinch bugs won't be your only targets of revenge: Dursban also kills fleas and ticks in your yard, and Diazinon is the chemical of choice for ants and June bug larvae. Always follow label directions.

When to suspect fungus:

• Grass will die irregularly, leaving islands of green, or green runners.

• This will occur mostly during the rainy season—though some people fight fungus all year long.

• If you inspect an affected grass blade, you may be able to see irregular black or rotting lesions.

To control fungus, spray an appropriate liquid fungicide, following label directions, on the surfaces of the leaves only. It is not necessary (or helpful) to penetrate the soil.

When to suspect grubs:

• Large birds may signal the presence of grubs by probing for them in your turf. For this reason, ecology-minded gardeners don't start using chemicals until the grubs become a real problem.

• Grubs eat roots. If you tug on a hand-ful of brown grass and it comes right out, grubs are the usual suspects.

To control grubs, make sure your Dursban or Diazinon spray penetrates deeply, or use granules according to label directions, and water in thoroughly. Grubs live well below the surface.

When to suspect army worms:

• Army worms are the terrorists of turf —ruthless destructive critters that don't know when to stop. They devour grass blades clear down to the rhizome, which is then scalded by the sun, leaving the grass completely helpless, sunburned and with no way to nourish itself.

• You'll see the scalped lawn, and, if you look more closely, you'll see the perpetrators themselves: lots of greenish brown worms 1/2-inch to an inch long. If you care enough to look really closely, you can even see their round green droppings.

To control, spray grass leaf surfaces with Dursban or Diazinon, following label directions. The same treatment can be used to control sod webworms, which are somewhat less common in South Florida.

For lots more about pests and how to control them, see "Wild Things: Insects, Fungus, and Weeds," starting on page 117.

Making Plants Grow: Nutrition, Nutrition, Nutrition

efore the tourists, long before developers, before the pioneers and the great Miccosukee nation that makes the Everglades its home, even before the first explorers, the native plants were thriving in South Florida. Perfectly adapted, they grabbed onto the rocky, sandy, difficult soils; clung to bark and branches; lifted themselves out of hostile waters on fantastic arching roots; and culled from the environment all the nourishment they needed.

So well did they thrive that early settlers could scarcely hack their way through the dense subtropical forests that covered coral ridges and hardwood hammocks unclaimed by nearly impenetrable Everglades wetlands.

Immigrants were amazed at the tropical bounty—they figured anything could grow in this paradise. It didn't take long to discover their mistake. Through the years, South Florida gardeners have learned that if we want our garden plants to thrive, we have to help. A lot. In fact, you won't go wrong to think of South Florida gardening as virtual hydroponics, and commit yourself to adding most, if not all, the nutrition your plants need.

Harold knows a gardener who, having

moved to South Florida from the rich river-bottom soils of the Midwest, sent a soil sample back to his trusted Illinois county agent to find out what nutritional supplements he would need to add. The analysis that came back was straightforward: "The only things your soil doesn't need," it said, "are sand and rock."

Actually the "rock" in our soil is oolite (pronounced oh-oh-lite) or oolitic limestone, which is made of pulverized, cemented fragments of inorganic limestone, and has nothing whatever to do with coral, though it's widely known as coral rock.

Oolite is the underlying foundation of Dade and Monroe Counties. In wet areas, you'll find muck, the organic surface material of the Everglades. The rest of South Florida gardens mostly in sand. Here and there, some gardeners are lucky enough to garden in marl—a claylike gray soil made of calcium carbonate, sand, and a little organic matter formed by microscopic organisms that lived in the shallows. Beneath the marl is usually oolite. All South Florida soils attest to the area's prehistory beneath the sea.

Nutrition is the single most important factor in successful South Florida gardening. A well-fed plant is a robust plant, a faster growing, better blooming plant, a plant better prepared to fend off the effects of extreme heat, drought, high wind, sudden cold, disease, and onslaughts of insects. If you learn from *The Art of South Florida Gardening* only one thing, Harold says, learn how to properly nourish your plants. This knowledge will be worth the price of the entire book.

Plant physiology 101

To you, the importance of a plant's leaves has to do with esthetics: how they make the plant look in your garden, how they blend and contrast with the leaves of other plants. To the plant, leaves are a tad more vital. Leaves are the part of the plant that process elements the plant absorbs from its environment (including the fertilizer you provide) into food it can use. Astonishingly, most of what the plant needs comes straight out of the air. Our job as gardeners is to ensure it has access to the rest.

Fertilizer sprinkled on the ground does the plant not a bit of good—until it dissolves, in rain water or water from a hose or sprinkler, into a liquid the roots can absorb. From the roots, this nutrient-rich liquid rises through the living plant tissue by the powerful force of transpirational pull: As molecules of water are transpired into the air as vapor, molecules below are drawn up to take their place. Assisted by the upward force of hydrostatic pressure and by osmosis, the process by which a liquid (nutrient-packed water) moves through a semipermeable membrane (a plant cell) into a denser liquid (the cell sap), transpirational pull pumps gallon upon gallon of liquid inexorably upward to the topmost leaf-tips of the tallest trees.

The essential leaf

Plants cannot live without leaves. To prove leaves are fundamental, next time you have a stump that keeps sprouting, don't use chemicals to kill it, just keep kicking off the new leaves as soon as they emerge. It might take several months or a year, but if you deprive the stump of leaves, it will die.

Green means grow, white means slow

Variegation—the white stripes, spots, and splashes on some plants' leaves—can give a leaf a lovely look, but the trade-off is slower growth. Less green in a leaf is a tip-off that there's less chlorophyll, a prime ingredient in a plant's food recipe. Variegated plants can also be more prone to fungus attack than all-green ones.

Nutrients are distributed throughout the leaves, where photosynthesis—the mysterious action of light energy on carbon dioxide, other gases, water, and the plant's own chlorophyll—converts the nutrients into sugars, proteins, carbohydrates, enzymes, acids, minerals, and other food elements the plant needs, to be distributed back down through the plant, all the way to the tips of the roots that collected the nutrients at the start.

In some cases, food produced by a plant's leaves nourish people, too. When we eat the collard or the tomato or the tangerine or the banana, we derive essential sugars, proteins, minerals, and other elements as surely as the plant did, so closely are our biologies related. Even those who eat meat are partaking of the foods produced by the plants the animals grazed on. Ultimately, all food used on earth is originally produced in the leaves of plants.

Be kind to your cambium

The living tissue of any dicotyledonous plant, even the largest tree, is contained in and adjacent to an extraordinarily thin green layer just under the outermost bark or sheath. This is the cambium layer, which separates the plant's inner heartwood and outer sapwood, through which xylem (*zy-lem*) and phloem (*flowm*)—think of veins and arteries—transport nutrients up from the roots and processed food elements down from the leaves.

The division and multiplication of cells in the cambium layer is what increases the thickness of the plant's trunk and stems. The rings in a cross-section of a tree are their footprints. In monocotyledonous plants, the vascular system is not concentrated in a single encasing layer, but is scattered in long bundles throughout the plant structure. Hack off a banana stalk and you'll find not rings, but a cross section view of these bundles.

Girdling a plant—cutting through its cambium layer all the way around—is an almost sure way to kill it. The roots will continue to absorb nutrients, which will continue to be sent up to the leaves, but the food the leaves produce will never again be able to travel back down beyond the girdling. If the plant can't quickly put out leaves below it, it's a goner. This is why lawnmowers and string trimmers should be kept well away from plants. You'd be surprised how many full-grown trees have been cut down by lawn-mowers. Up north, animals like rabbits and deer often girdle trees when they feed—it's part of nature's thinning process. Beavers do it on purpose. They need the wood.

Note to pet owners

Cambium layer damage can be done by the chain with which you attach the family dog to a tree. If Bowzer can't live in the house with you, which is what he'd prefer, better to get a special purpose sheathed wire hoop for the tree and clip the dog's lead line to that. Better yet, install a fence. The tree—and the dog—will be much happier.

The importance of being watered

A happy plant is a turgid plant: Its living cells are full of water. Plants should always be turgid when they are fed. When a cell is empty, it literally collapses —and the plant wilts. The last thing a wilted plant wants is fertilizer. What it wants is a good, deep watering. To be sure your plants are turgid when you feed them, always water the day before you fertilize.

Surplus food and water are stored in the plant's living tissue (think of water-retaining cactus, virtually all stem) against times when food may be scarce. This is why some tree rings are narrow and some are wide. Wide indicates a year of good nutrition and robust growth. Narrow indicates slimmer pickings. Regularly fertilized plants can keep plenty of energy in reserve, so they'll be able to sprout new growth if they undergo a trauma like blowing over in a storm or being hat racked by a self-styled "tree surgeon" with a chain saw. Feeding a plant regularly before you prune it enables it to build up its energy reserves to prepare for the shock to come. If you prune first, you'll have a very frustrated plant, dutifully pumping nutrient-rich liquid up through its tissues —with no leaves there to process it. If you make this mistake, wait until the plant draws on reserve energy to push out a few new leaves, and feed it again. The plant will forgive you, just this once.

Learning your N-P-Ks

By Florida law, every package of garden fertilizer sold in the state must wear a label describing its contents. Most fertilizers contain three major elements: Nitrogen (chemical symbol N; derived from various sources), Phosphorus (P; from phosphoric acid), and Potassium (K; from potash).

Nitrogen promotes healthy growth of green tissue like leaves and stems. Phosphorus is found in plant cell structure and fruit. Potassium boosts a plant's immune system, helps in the production of flowers and fruit, and encourages healthy roots and stems.

A bag of fertilizer is usually marked with three large numbers, maybe 6-6-6 or 28-4-4 or 2-8-10. These numbers tell you the percent by weight of each major element, always in the same order—nitrogen, phosphorus, and potassium. In a 100-pound bag of 10-10-10, for example, you'd get 10 pounds each of nitrogen, phosphorus, and potassium. If it's 2-8-10, there are two pounds of nitrogen, eight of phosphorus, and 10 of potassium.

The rest of the weight is accounted for by the compounds in which the chemicals are found, and in some cases by inert carriers that allow the active ingredients to be distributed evenly and in the proper concentration.

A balanced fertilizer, one whose N-P-K numbers are equal (10-10-10, 8-8-8, or the ever-popular 6-6-6), delivers equal amounts of each element, for balanced greening, growth, and flower or fruit production.

Other fertilizers are formulated for specialized purposes. For instance, since grass has little in the way of roots, and flowers are not an issue, most chemical lawn fertilizers are much higher in nitrogen than ones meant for other plants.

Milorganite (6-2-0), a slow-acting organic fertilizer excellent for lawns, has no potassium at all. A fertilizer for a fruit tree or flowering shrub might have a 2-8-10 formula, low on the nitrogen and higher in potassium so the plant won't waste its time making impressive leaves when what you want is lots of gardenias or grapefruit.

Many fertilizers contain other nutrients, including minor elements, along with the

---

Don't move the mulch

No need to remove mulch before applying granular fertilizer. Just sprinkle it right on top and water it in. Once dissolved, the fertilizer will wash through the mulch and into the ground. The microorganisms in the mulch, busy breaking down the organic material, may use up some of the nitrogen in your fertilizer in the process, so it's a good idea to add some extra nitrogen from time to time.

When the old broken down mulch needs to be replaced, don't throw it away. Just loosen it up a bit before you add a new layer. It will enrich the soil with organic material and valuable nutrients plants can use.

N-P-K. Some are specially formulated for the alkaline soils found in much of South Florida.

If the right fertilizer doesn't happen to be on hand, however, Harold says you can probably get away with using what you have. What's important is that the plant be fed. In a pinch, Harold has used rose fertilizer on his tomatoes and citrus fertilizer on his caladiums. Virtually any fertilizer, he contends, is better than no fertilizer.

As with any other product, fertilizer quality should be considered. High quality fertilizer, which typically has more insoluble nitrogen and less chlorine—an ingredient many experts say should not account for more than a few percent of your fertilizer, dissolves more slowly, so its effects endure. The tag will tell you how much of the fertilizer's nitrogen is soluble and how much is insoluble. Check, for example, the source of the nitrogen. Lawn food with a high percentage of urea, an extremely soluble man-made nitrogen fixed into pellets, will green your lawn fast but to short-lived effect. To a plant, this would be something like having a 12-course meal on Sunday and following up with a week of fasting.

Nitrogen derived from insoluble urea formaldehyde, on the other hand, breaks down more slowly, seeping into the soil in more moderate amounts, maintaining the green longer. This doesn't mean 45-0-0 soluble urea isn't beneficial in its place. Commercial nurseries use it by the ton to green up their plants and make other chemicals work more efficiently. For normal gardening purposes, though, the more insoluble nitrogen, the better. High quality fertilizers can be more expensive per pound, but since they usually provide better, longer lasting nutrition, they can be a better value in the long run.

Fluid food

Some fertilizers come in crystals especially formulated to be dissolved in water and applied as liquid drenches or foliar sprays. Popular ones are Peter's, Miracle-Gro, and Rapid Gro. Some liquid fertilizers are already dissolved and ready to be applied, but this questionable convenience can be very expensive, considering you're being charged for the packaging and transport of the water in which the fertilizer is dissolved. Harold uses his own water.

N-P-K numbers on these water-soluble fertilizers are often quite high (20-20-20, 15-30-15), but, when the correct amount is diluted according to package directions, the resulting concentration is so weak that giving the plant

How to use a hose-end sprayer

A hose-end sprayer—a jar with a hose attachment on one side of its lid and an adjustable spray nozzle on the other— makes short work of applying the correct amounts of foliar sprays and other chemicals.

Its chemical container is a proportioning jar, usually marked in fluid ounces as well as gallons. If it's not, remember this: 1 fluid ounce = 2 tablespoons.

You pour in the concentrate to the mark for the correct number of ounces (or spoon in a corresponding number of tablespoons), and fill with plain water to the mark for the correct number of gallons. The water from the hose, rushing through the jar's lid, will siphon the liquid from the jar, delivering the proper proportion of nutritional elements to your plant.

too much is rarely a problem. For some applications, half-strength is recommended in the instructions. Soluble fertilizers come in various formulations, from balanced general purpose to special recipes for orchids, acid-loving plants, lawns, foliar feeding, and other applications.

Soluble fertilizer can be thought of as baby food for plants. Since it's already dissolved when you drench the soil, roots immediately lap it up. And since it's in so gentle a concentration, you can use it right after planting and as often as you like—even every few days if the spirit moves you—to encourage new plants or coddle those you feel need a bit of extra attention. Liquid fertilizer is ideal for potted plants and plants hanging in trees, as long as you apply it frequently. Harold says if you use liquid fertilizers once a year, you may as well not use it at all. Once every couple of weeks is much more effective.

Soluble crystals should always be measured and mixed according to the directions on the label. If the directions say one tablespoon per gallon, use one tablespoon. Even a little more might be a little more than your plant can stand.

The organics

Organic fertilizers deliver the same nitrogen, phosphorus, and potassium as chemical fertilizers, but they do so in natural soil conditioners, and usually in much lower amounts. Instead of inert carrier, the carrier is organic, which actively treats the soil with  beneficial microorganisms. The most widely used organics are the various animal manures and processed, activated sewage sludge, among the best known of which is Milorganite.

Fresh manures are, chemically speaking, quite hot, and must be composted or aged (allowed to break down into soil-like particles) before use to prevent burning plants. The kind of cow manure that you purchase in sacks is almost always composted.

If you want to use chicken manure right off the farm, be sure to ask whether the manure was sprayed with boron to kill insects. If it was, pass on the manure. Boron is necessary to plants only in minuscule amounts; too high a dose of it can be deadly.

Some gardeners swear by Milorganite for feeding their lawns. Harold uses it for his. Applied according to package directions in spring, summer, and fall, it releases its nutrients at a slow, steady pace year-round. Because the activity of organics slows during the cooler months, you may wish to give your lawn an extra winter boost with a chemical fertilizer the first year or two. Over the course of a few years, the benefits of an organic fertilizing program become more and more apparent. And because it doesn't burn, you can spread it around anytime it's convenient for you, and just wait for the rain to wash it in.

Special diets

A South Florida garden might have 50 kinds of plants, each with its own cultural background, a whole set of environmental expectations, and certain special requirements. Yet we plant them all together and say "grow." While most plants, aiming to please, grow just fine on a regular schedule of high-quality balanced fertilizer, some really prefer special diets. Manufacturers are more than happy to oblige, by providing fertilizers with specific, specially proportioned ingredients for virtually every plant you own.

When young plants of all kinds are getting established for the first year or two, they seem to do best on frequent small applications of a balanced fertilizer. Once they mature, their dietary preferences diverge. Citrus trees favor fruit tree special. Mangos and avocados have a formulation just for them. Gardenias and ixoras prefer acid-forming fertilizers to keep their leaves green. Palms crave manganese and magnesium, which they get in the proper formulation in a good palm special. There are specific fertilizers for orchids, crotons, roses, and vegetable gardens. You can even purchase fertilizer ingredients separately and mix your own.

Some gardeners switch formulations from time to time, or vary their plants' diets between granules and liquids or between chemical and organic. This way they make sure their plants get everything they need and never get tired of the menu.

Vitamins for plants

There's more alphabet to this soup than N-P-K, however. Looking further down the package or tag, you'll see other elements, and more numbers. These include the minor elements plants need—but in such vanishingly small amounts they're also called secondary, trace, and micro-elements. Think of them as vitamins for your plants.

Like vitamins for people, some of these elements can be toxic if used incorrectly. Some need to be taken in combination with others to facilitate their absorption, while the wrong mix can actually block absorption. If the soil is too alkaline, iron and some other minerals can chemically bond with molecules in the soil, tying them up and rendering them unavailable for absorption by the plant's roots.

For all these complicated reasons, it may make sense to apply most micro-nutrients directly to leaves and green tissues rather than as a soil drench. If the elements don't go into the ground, they can't be affected by what they encounter there. Various formulations of minor elements—general purpose, citrus special, and others—can be found bottled at garden stores, ready to dilute to the proper proportions and apply to your trees and shrubs. Plants requiring no distinctive formulation need be given only the equivalent of an all-purpose vitamin tablet—a good general nutritional spray.

Try to spray the more absorbent undersides of the leaves rather than the less penetrable upper surfaces. Liquid just runs right off waxy leaves like citrus. Some people find it helps to use a specially bottled spreader-sticker (surfactant), sold in garden centers, to keep the sprayed chemical on the leaves. Some add a drop of liquid detergent to accomplish the same thing. For best effect, nutritional spray should be used three times a year, in spring, summer, and fall—about the time you do your regular fertilizing. Always follow the directions on the label.

A mineral menu

Magnesium (Mg). Found in chlorophyll, magnesium is the substance that makes plants green. Magnesium is absorbed mostly through a plant's roots.

Manganese (Mn). Often deficient in sandy soils, and South Florida's alkaline soils tie it up, rendering it unavailable through the roots. Manganese can be absorbed directly into the leaves.

Copper (Cu). The symptoms of copper deficiency can be confused with those caused by an excess of nitrogen—elongated leaves, thin, too rapid growth. When used in foliar spray, copper also acts as a fungicide. Copper is

114

toxic to bromeliads, including Spanish moss. If spray containing copper must be used around bromeliads, they should be rinsed with clear water immediately afterward.

Zinc (Zn). Necessary to the production of plant enzymes. Can be absorbed through leaves. Zinc deficiency causes leaves to elongate and turn yellow (chlorotic).

Iron (Fe). Allows enzymes to work properly. Deficiency causes leaves to yellow between green veins. Iron can be applied as foliar spray or, when chelated (pronounced *key*-layted)—combined with other molecules so it can't bond with elements in the soil—as a soil drench.

Sulfur (S). Helps make soil more acidic (tends to lower pH). Well-fed plants obtain it from the sulfates in their regular fertilizer.

Calcium (Ca). Makes soil more alkaline. Sometimes, vegetable rot can be alleviated by the addition of lime (calcium) to the soil. For this reason, some gardeners mix a little dry milk powder into the soil around their tomato plants.

When to fertilize

At planting time. Organic fertilizers—activated sludge or well-composted manure—may be mixed in with the soil in a planting hole or incorporated into the planting bed before you put in plants. This cannot be done with chemical fertilizers, which can burn tender new roots.

After you plant or transplant. Because newly installed plants are able to use only small amounts of fertilizer, they need to be fed often. Liquid fertilizer applied at least weekly for a few months gives them a good start, followed by monthly small applications of granular fertilizer until the plant is established.

For hanging baskets, potted plants, ferns, and plants in trees. Use liquid fertilizer at least every two weeks, or toss in a handful of

How to fertilize a tree

Have you ever seen someone sprinkle granular fertilizer right next to a tree's trunk? It doesn't occur to them that the roots adjacent to the trunks of most trees (palms are a notable exception) are mainly for support, and that most of the feeder roots are out under the ends of the branches and beyond, in the area called the drip line.

In the recommended amount for your size tree (the package will guide you), the fertilizer should be sprinkled in a band a couple of feet wide all around the drip line so that, watered in, the nutrients will filter down through the soil to the feeder roots. Remember that nutrients dissipate quickly through porous soils, so must be replenished every few months.

A word about tree spikes: Useless. Equally useless, and potentially harmful, is the process of drilling holes in the ground around your tree and filling them with fertilizer. Drilling damages roots; since a tree can't search for fertilizer, its roots will stumble upon your spike or fertilizer column by chance. The concentrated fertilizer can burn the delicate feeder roots, and your tree will think it has hit Chernobyl.

If tree spikes are the only fertilizer you have, Harold's advice is to crumble them up and sprinkle them on the ground around the drip line (water well).

Milorganite every two or three months, or use a gentle, encapsulated time-release fertilizer like Osmocote. Follow label directions.

For lawns and established trees and shrubs. Granular fertilizer should be applied three times a year—spring, summer, and fall. Because nutrients filter down through our rocky, sandy soils, they must be replenished regularly to avoid the feast-and-famine effects of infrequent fertilizing. Foliar nutritional sprays should be used three times a year, too.

For a tree or plant that's not doing well. Extra attention is in order. Frequent, small applications of fertilizer, watered well before and after, will help nourish it back to health. Then it can be put back on the regular three-times-a-year routine. Some gardeners kill their plants with kindness, watering too much and using too much fertilizer per application. For plants, just as for people, regular light meals are far more restorative.

For all plants. Always water a day before you fertilize.

Wild Things: Insects, Fungus, and Weeds

garden is a miniature ecosystem, teeming with life. Marvelous birds, butterflies, lizards, and bees may all make their homes in your garden. So may helpful frogs, spiders, snakes, and earthworms. Unfortunately, ants, fleas, plant-eating bugs, unwelcome fungi, and untamed plants we call weeds probably do, too.

Back in the days before garden stores, gardeners were prepared to mix their own organic remedies to deal with unwelcome pests, or purchase them at the local drug or feed stores. Harold's father used to soak his cigar butts in a bucket, strain off the tobacco "tea," fill his Flit gun, and spray. The nicotine-sulfate-rich potion killed most garden pests—including aphids and beetles.

You could make your own tobacco tea today, or purchase the same highly toxic chemical in a product called Black Leaf 40, an organic substance which kills the same range of bugs. Garlic water has also been shown to be a potent organic insecticide, and a commercially packaged version is being market-tested. An advantage of organic toxins is that insects do not normally become immune to them, as they often do to synthetic chemicals.

One of the first synthetic garden chemicals was the infamous DDT. DDT was considered the model of a good pesticide back then: highly potent, with a long-term residual kill. It's still one of the world's most widely used insecticides, but was banned in the United States when its lethal abilities were found to go well beyond bugs. As new environmental evidence turned up, basic thinking about garden insecticides changed. Now we want chemicals that kill quickly and dissipate fast. Malathion and Dursban are such chemicals.

Over the years, a great many agricultural and garden chemicals have been taken off the market. Fewer and fewer chemicals, even if approved for use by specially trained and equipped professionals, are permitted for home use. When fungicide licenses expire, they are seldom renewed. Soil fumigants are no longer available to home gardeners. Scarcely any miticides remain, and those are so costly that gardeners have had to start forming consortiums to buy them. New products have become more and more difficult to license—often harder than pharmaceuticals. This is because the residual effects of a substance applied to plant material or garden soil might show up long after the fact, indirectly, and remote from the site of application, making them extremely difficult and time-consuming to assess.

Come into my parlor . . .

Impelled by governmental restrictions (and, dare it be hoped, at least partly motivated by environmental concerns), the agricultural chemical industry has crossed an important threshold of ecological sensitivity, and seems to be re-evaluating its mission. Researchers studying "bio controls" ask questions like: If a spider can use the most minuscule amount of its venom to dispatch its prey, yet leave it edible, and presumably palatable, why can't we synthesize this substance to make a garden insecticide? Some researchers are working at doing just that.

Genetic engineers pursue other avenues. Implanting a gene from a bacterium called *Bacillus thurigenensis* (BT) in a tobacco plant gene was found to render the tobacco plant toxic to its formidable enemy, the tobacco worm. It was then implanted in corn to fight off the corn root worm. BT can now be purchased in sprays called Thuricide and Dipel, which are formulated specifically to kill worms and caterpillars in home gardens.

Scientists are attempting similar genetic adjustments to the DNA of tomatoes and other edible plants. The hope is that many of the vegetables in our supermarkets and plants we purchase for home gardening may eventually be able physiologically to shrug off what bugs them without outside help.

While we're waiting, the trend toward using fewer chemicals, and less often, seems irreversible. Eco-conscious gardeners no longer reach for the sprayer at the first sign of a chewed leaf. If they must use chemical controls, they do so intelligently, practicing the home-gardening version of the newest approach to commercial pest control, integrated pest management. In commercial IPM, highly paid specialists monitor the fields and do spot counts of insect populations. Steps are taken only when populations reach pre-determined levels. You can keep an eye on your "fields" in much the same way, for free.

Bearing in mind that at best we can control pests, never eliminate them, here are some guidelines to intelligent pest control:

Be sure of the problem

If you're not familiar with the symptoms that confront you, you might easily mistake wind damage for insect damage, or a mineral deficiency for a fungus or other disease. Further investigation and a trip to a gardening expert, leaf or stem in hand, may be warranted.

Use the correct remedy

If sucking insects have infested your orange tree, chemicals meant to kill chewing insects will only amuse the little suckers.

Start with your least toxic weapons

Lady bug larvae eat aphids by the thousands. They may be able to keep your aphid population within bearable limits. If the lady bugs need help, there are nontoxic things you can do before reaching for the chemical can. For starters, you can blast the aphids off your plants with the garden hose. You may have to reblast in a couple of days, but this approach is much more healthful for the lady bugs (which are killed by the same spray that kills the aphids), better for the environment, and lots less expensive than chemicals.

You can also pinch or snip off the bug-covered growing tips and toss them into the trash. The plant will probably look better after the trimming, too.

If you have an overpowering desire to spray something, a solution of a couple of tablespoons of liquid soap mixed into a gallon of water and sprayed on the leaves suffocates aphids.

If all these ecologically sound remedies fail, and you need to resort to chemicals, start with the one least damaging to you, the plant, and the environment.

Mix only the amount you intend to use

Try not to have chemical mixture left over. Most mixed sprays gradually lose their potency anyway, so are not worth keeping for next time. Leftover chemicals poured on the ground can soak into our drinking water supply. They shouldn't be poured anywhere else, either. Better to use them up.

Liquid chemicals meant to be diluted with water are easiest to mix. Wettable powders can be tricky and, incompletely mixed, can clog a sprayer. If powder is all you can find, Harold says you can make the smoothest possible mixture by first adding just a little water to the correct amount of powder, making a sort of slurry. Then mix in the rest of the water a little at a time.

Follow directions as if your health depended on it

Chemical labels are full of long-winded health and safety cautions and warnings

mandated by the government, usually printed in type so small you need binoculars to read them. Sometimes you dutifully plow through all the verbiage only to be referred to additional accompanying pamphlets for the information you're really after: how much chemical to use per gallon of water and per square foot of garden. If you have trouble finding these instructions, keep searching. If you still can't find it, take the trouble to ask. You can reasonably expect a chemical to work as advertised only when mixed and applied according to the maker's recommendations.

Pulling your weight

Even if you need more than a gallon of spray, you can still use a one-gallon sprayer. Just mix the additional amount in a separate container. When the sprayer is empty, reload with your reserves. Even if you have a larger sprayer, it still might be more comfortable to carry a gallon at a time, since a gallon weighs half as much as two.

For obvious reasons of health and safety, be sure to carefully label and identify the contents of all containers, and never use water or food containers to store garden chemicals.

Use the proper applicator

This doesn't have to be fancy. For small jobs it might be a plastic bottle with a hand trigger top. For a few dozen shrubs, a one-gallon pump sprayer comes in handy. For lawns, you'll need a hose-end sprayer to deliver the large amounts of mixture required to saturate the soil (hose-end sprayers can propel solution into treetops, too).

Some people still swear by the type of old-fashioned trombone sprayer Harold's father used to use: three feet of brass tubing with a rubber hose that leads down to a bucket of mixed chemical solution. This home-built-looking contraption can deliver a gentle spray or shoot a jet of water 30 feet into the branches of a tree —and either build up your muscles or put your arm in a sling.

B-r-r-r-r-r-!

If you use aerosol insecticides, be sure to keep the can at least 18 inches from foliage. The spray can be cold!

It's very clear

When you spray a clear liquid, it's not easy to tell if the sprayer has clogged and you're studiously applying pure water. Try adding a drop of food color to the proportioning jar so you can see what you're spraying.

Wear protective gear

Chemicals are no joke. Sprays meant to kill insects might not kill a human being outright (though some can, and have, as occasional news stories about some commercial practices attest), but breathing them and having them on your skin regularly, over time, can't do you any good.

Depending on the chemicals in question, those who want to be safe wear protection such as rubber gloves, long sleeves, goggles, and paper breathing filters.

Practice good technique

How the chemical is applied can be as important as what is applied. For best effect, most liquid chemicals should be sprayed until "runoff"—until the liquid starts to run off the leaf. Some should be lightly misted onto the leaves. Check the product label to be sure. With most chemicals, it's usually smartest to aim upward toward the leaves' tender undersides, whose surfaces are more penetrable to sprays — and where insects think they can hide.

For safety, don't let spray drift back on you, your neighbor's car, or sensitive plants, and please don't let it settle on nearby fish ponds or bird baths. It could result in a deadly cocktail.

Take care of your equipment

Sprayers and measuring equipment should be thoroughly washed and rinsed each time you use them. This helps guard against clogging and corrosion, as well as prevent residual chemicals from being inadvertently mixed together. Some people give everything a final rinse with baking soda just to be sure.

Neither fertilizers, fungicides, insecticides, nor anything else should be used in equipment you've used for herbicides, no matter how well you've cleaned it. Have a separate sprayer, boldly marked, for weed killers only.

All gardening equipment and supplies should be kept well out of reach of children and pets. Remember: It's all poison.

[Note: All chemical and brand names in this book were available for home gardening use at the time of printing. Things change. If necessary, ask a trusted garden chemical retailer for equivalent substitutes, or call your county agent, whose address and phone number you'll find at the back of this book.]

Don't shoot!

One of the biggest, ugliest, most frightful looking worms you're likely to find in a South Florida garden is the Orange Dog caterpillar, found mostly on citrus trees. Its brown and white camouflage makes it look exactly like a bird dropping with orange antennae, and does an excellent job of protecting it from its natural enemies.

You, of course, will not be fooled. Not only is an Orange Dog an ugly monster, it is apt to eat more than a few leaves. You will be tempted to nuke it.

But if you restrain yourself, and let it have the leaves, soon this horrid creature will spin a cocoon, from which it will emerge as the wonder it was destined to be: a Giant Swallowtail butterfly, yellow and black with a six-inch wingspan — one of the most beautiful creatures to be found in a South Florida garden.

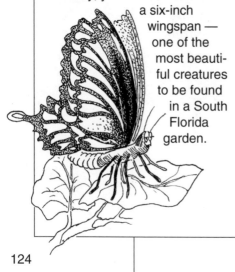

How to cure what you've got: Insects

Chewing insects

Chewing insects comprise a crowded category that includes beetles, worms, maggots, grubs, caterpillars, grasshoppers, and other bad-news bugs. Slugs and snails also chew, though they're not insects, but mollusks, related to clams and oysters. The modern approach is to try to recognize that a few chewed leaves are not a national disaster. However, if your observations tell you the beasties are chewing more than their share, you'll want to close the cafe.

Chewing insects are dispatched with stomach poisons, and they must ingest the substance in order for it to work. Sevin is thought of as the environmentally safest of these chemical insecticides. It can be used in liquid spray form or in a direct light dusting of powdered material. Because Sevin is bad news for bees, it should be applied only late in the evening, after the bees have gone to bed. If Sevin won't do the trick, try a more potent broad-spectrum killer like Dursban or Diazinon (the main ingredient in Spectracide). Diazinon also kills a sucking insect called scale.

Grubs live underground as beetle larvae, spending their time happily chewing tender roots while waiting to win their wings. You might see a few—inch-long curled white uglies with brown tips—when you dig holes for plants. If crows and other large birds appear on your lawn in Alfred Hitchcockian numbers, and no film crews are in the area, it may be a sign grubs are on the menu. Wait awhile. The birds may take care of them for you. If they don't, Dursban or Diazinon drenches should. Note to fishermen: Grubs make good bait.

Worms and caterpillars (moth and butterfly larvae) usually hatch on the stems and leaves on which their eggs were deposited, and where they'll make their homes and take their meals until they die or weave cocoons. If you want to get rid of them, you can often pick them off by hand. If there are too many for this, the biological controls Dipel or Thuricide (BT) can be tried before resorting to harsher remedies.

If you like having butterflies in your garden and don't want to eliminate their larvae, the National Audubon Society's *Guide to North American Butterflies* is a small handbook with good photos to help you identify them.

Snails and slugs (you know they're there by their glistening trails) do their best work in the dark, and a single night-shift of snails or slugs can make Swiss cheese of a whole bed of plants. During the day, they burrow down in the mulch.

The organic control is to dig a plastic bowl or wide-mouth jar into the ground so its opening is at ground level, and fill it with beer. When the critters stop off for a short one on their way to work, they'll die happy. If the beer doesn't do them in, try snail and slug bait—just a little; they can't eat much and they like it fresh —can be slipped under a piece of wood in a shaded area. The offenders will be attracted to the bait, and will appreciate having a nice cozy place to sleep. What they won't know is that this time, it's the big sleep.

Grasshoppers. A few grasshoppers in a garden can be entertaining, and the big fellows—dressed in bright colors and as long as three inches overall—are quite handsome. Too many, though, and you'd better do something about them or they'll have your garden for lunch.

Grasshoppers like to bury their eggs adjacent to their favorite foods, some of which are amaryllis and lilies—crinum, spider, and others. When still small (the immature black and orange stage), grasshoppers will succumb to the same chemicals that get rid of other chewing insects. But once they reach the big, colorful, lubber stage, they must be captured by hand and mechanically dispatched. Harold has spent many an afternoon, over the years, dancing about, trying to outwit—or outlast—marauding grasshoppers. More forgiving gardeners pay for their benevolence with decimated lily beds.

Sucking insects

Sucking insects have few, if any, redeeming qualities. They cripple leaves by draining the juice out of them. They can also spread virus—a sucking insect was the vector of the lethal yellowing plasma that killed South Florida's coconut tree population. The harm sucking insects can do to your plants dwarfs chewing insects' taking of a few leaves. Nip these guys early—in the bud, if you must.

The perpetrators—scales, aphids, mealy bugs, white flies, and mites (mites are not technically insects, but the black sheep of the spider family)—that can do such widespread damage are so tiny they are usually convicted on circumstantial evidence. Black sooty mold on leaves and stems is an almost certain indication of the presence of a sucking insect. The sooty mold is a harmless fungus that grows on the insects' secretions (called honeydew). Ants like honeydew, too, and in fact have discovered that they can herd aphids around a plant like honeydew-dairy cows, and even milk them. So if you see a lot of ants running around your plants, along with the sooty mold, evidence mounts of the presence of sucking insects.

Sucking insects reproduce rapidly. Because most insecticides do not kill the eggs, directions usually advise spraying three times about a week apart to kill the successive generations of new hatchlings. Two *contact* killers used to control most sucking insects are Malathion (synthetic) and Black Leaf 40 (organic).

Systemic sprays can also be very effective when properly used. Systemic chemicals penetrate the vegetative tissues, making the plant itself poisonous to the insect that sucks it. Such a readily absorbed substance just about mandates wearing protective clothing while you apply it and that you be especially attentive to the directions. Equipment should be meticulously cleaned after being used for

Chemical storage

Air can quickly neutralize a garden chemical. Among the best ways to store opened containers of fertilizers, fungicides, insecticides, and herbicides is to put them in air-tight plastic canisters or zip-lock bags. Mark containers carefully with contents and directions.

Not for hibiscus

While Malathion is (as of this writing) a recommended chemical for sucking insects, it should not be used on hibiscus plants. Try systemic remedies instead.

systemics. Harold recommends against using systemic insecticides on anything edible, at least until after the crop has been harvested. Check label directions for specific cautions.

Aphids are about 1/16" long, come in various shades of green, black, and brown, and tend to colonize around plants' newly opening buds and growing tips. If the aphids are unchecked, leaves and buds may begin to deform. Aphids can be washed off with a stiff stream from a garden hose. Repeat every few days until the problem is gone. Soapsuds suffocate aphids; so do commercially bottled insecticidal soaps like Safer's, and Volck oil or "summer oil" spray, a horticultural oil (Volck oil is temperature sensitive, so do read the label).

Scales are much more menacing than aphids, and more difficult to control. Scales look like minuscule barnacles in brown, red, grey, black, or white, found affixed to stems, twigs, and the undersides of leaves. Their larvae crawl around the plant until they find a spot to their liking away from the glare of publicity. When they reach the age of consent, they anchor themselves permanently and get down to the business of serious sucking and egg laying.

Most scales are tiny, about 1/8 inch long. Some, like the white and orange cottony cushiony scale often found on podocarpus plants, can be the size of an aspirin. Snow scale, which attacks hibiscus, is so small it resembles a coating of confectioner's sugar; you might mistake it for mildew or fungus. How to tell: When crushed, scale is gooey when alive, crispy when dead.

Scales are practically born pregnant, reproducing with such alacrity that large colonies can appear seemingly overnight. They also have tough outer shells that contact sprays have a hard time penetrating. Systemics are most effective against them, especially on grassy-looking plants like liriope, under whose slender, thickly arranged leaves it can be hard to spray.

Mealy bugs win the most common pest award for plants indoors and on screened-in patios. This is because, living indoors, they have no enemies—except you. A mealy bug looks just like the end of a Q-Tip, a white blob tucked down where a leaf joins the stem. It spins webbing around itself for protection, and moves almost imperceptibly around the plant. Most attack foliage; some cagily attach themselves at the base of the plant, below soil level where you can't see. Palm growers take note: Mealy bugs have a particular fondness for chamadorea palms. They are very difficult to penetrate with contact chemicals. Systemics will clean them out better and faster.

> ### Counter-resistance
>
> Since fungi and insects can develop resistance or immunity to garden chemicals, it helps to alternate chemicals from month to month, or, for some applications (fungicides on roses, for instance), to spray a couple of kinds in combination.

If you prefer not to use chemicals, a small enough infestation of mealy bugs can be wiped out with a pad saturated with soapy water or alcohol. Some gardeners spray the alcohol directly on the bugs; they say it evaporates too quickly to harm the plant. Or you can try moving afflicted indoor plants to a shady area outdoors for a couple of weeks, to see if hungry critters will make a meal of the mealy bugs.

Chinch bugs love St. Augustine grass. They are controlled by soaking the ground several feet around the dead area with Dursban or Diazinon solution. (See "Grass with Class," page 87.)

Whiteflies, related to aphids and scales, do a lot of commercial crop damage and are very difficult to control. Young whiteflies are flat, oval, and wingless. After hatching, they move around on the plant, feeding on the undersides of leaves. Adult whiteflies are pure white, very tiny, and wildly active. Shake an infested bush—they seem to like caladiums, poinsettias, and aralias especially—and white nits fly around like dandruff. The undersides of affected leaves become silvery with white-fly cast-offs.

To control whitefly, county agents usually advise using Malathion in repeated applications. Volck oil spray is recommended for use on citrus trees. But the truth is white flies seem to be immune to just about everything.

Thrips are the small, dark, sliver-shaped flying insects commonly seen on gardenias. They are not usually a huge problem, and they can often be washed out with water. For chemical control, Malathion is recommended. Many orchid growers use the systemic chemical Orthene for thrips.

Other pests

In addition to chewing and sucking insects, from time to time your garden may be afflicted by other pesky critters.

Mites are tracked by the damage they do: bronzed, roughened leaf surfaces, and dry, curling leaves. The mites themselves are too infinitesimally small to see in action on the plant. On fast-growing plants you can try to prune off as much of the affected plant tissue as possible, and spray the rest carefully with a specially formulated miticide. Your mite-infested clippings should be packed into a plastic bag, sealed, and discarded. Mites are bad news for rose bushes. Though a small, new infestation can be knocked off like aphids with a sharp blast from the hose, a major mite problem can require an equally major investment in miticide.

Rasping insects file away green leaf tissues, leaving leaf-shaped skeletons; **tunnel-**

ing insects make meandering white paths through your leaves; **boring insects** drill stems and fruit; **fruit flies** lay eggs that hatch as maggots in your loquats and papayas. There's nothing much you can do about these except the plastic-bags-over-the-developing-fruit trick, to try to frustrate the flies.

Then there are the **mole crickets**, which can tunnel underneath a plant and pull the whole thing into the ground (mole cricket bait needed here); **ants** (Diazinon drench); and stinging, sometimes deadly, **fire ants** (controlled with bait-type products the worker ants feed to the queen). And there are whole families of different **nematodes**—microscopic parasites that suck a plant's roots—including hero nematodes that destroy their vicious cousins.

While it's a good idea to know about all these insects—there are excellent specialized books on the subject—and to know which weapons to use when you need them (the county agent can tell you), the best attitude is a relaxed one. Insect pests can never be eliminated from your garden ecology, only kept under reasonable control. If they get the best of you one season, Harold says, you can always have a rematch.

Fungus

Like it or not, the world is full of fungus. Some fungi, like white truffles and porcini mushrooms, are delicious (and expensive). Others are astonishingly large —a single organism can extend for miles just beneath the surface of the ground. Some, like penicillin, can actually save lives. Others are quite deadly. Many, even the deadly ones, are beautiful.

What you recognize as a fungus—

a toadstool, a bracket on the side of a palm, or the furry mold on a wet patch of mulch—is the fruiting part of the fungus. The rest of the organism is invisibly at work below the surface. In gardens, many types of fungi, including the mushrooms that pop up periodically, are nothing to worry about. They actually perform a valuable service down there in the dark, digesting nonliving vegetative material and mulch, helping turn it into the humus that enriches the soil for your plants. The fungi that give you grief are the kind that try to digest your living shrubs, trees, and lawn. Fortunately, these fungi, like insects and weeds, can be controlled. But, since fungal infections can't be cured, the control is prevention.

Fungi adore South Florida, especially in the high temperatures and humidity of summer. Give them some mulch piled snugly up against the trunk of a tree, and they will move right in. Water your lawn at night, and fungi will enjoy the moist warm splendor in your grass—and repay you by making large brown spots. What fungus doesn't like: Air circulation. Sunshine. Cleanliness. Robust, healthy plants. Take care of your plants with a good fertilization program, and they might grow right through a fungus problem. Plants under stress are most vulnerable to attack.

Frustrating the fungus

You rarely see fungus on a plant native to South Florida; that's a war natives have pretty much won. Some local South Florida vegetables have been scientifically bred to resist fungal diseases. One way to avoid fungus, therefore, is not to plant things noted for their susceptibility to fungal infections. The trouble is, fungus-vulnerable plants are often exactly the ones we want. For these plants, gardeners must be prepared to take some protective

Little garden do-gooders

Insecticides kill the good guys just as dead as the bad. Poisoned insects are, in turn, poisonous to the birds, lizards, snakes, and frogs that eat them. A good book on Florida insects can help you decide which you can tolerate—and may even want to encourage—in your garden. Here are some creatures you may welcome:

Lady bugs. The familiar small flying round orange domes with black spots (or black with red) are the adults. Their strange-looking mottled brownish spine-and-cone-covered larvae, which you hardly ever see because they dine at night, go after aphids with relish.

Lizards. As interesting as diminutive dinosaurs. They establish territories all through the garden, engage in dramatic rituals, and eat their share of flying pests.

Dragonflies and damselflies. Feed on annoy-ing bugs, and their larvae eat mosquito wigglers.

Snakes. The sort apt to be seen in domestic gardens are virtually always nonpoisonous and nonaggres-sive. Black garden snakes, with or without yellow necklaces, are common; they eat bugs, including roaches. Also common is the red rat snake (white with red spots), the only native American constrictor, which eats rodents. If you see a snake slithering through the grass or come upon one snoozing among your hanging baskets, it's only natural to react with a start. But you'd be wise to let it be, and appreciate it as part of the ecosystem of a healthy garden.

Earthworms are miniature biological earth-moving equipment, burrowing around under ground, aerating and conditioning the soil. Earthworm castings are sometimes sold as conditioned garden soil. An earthworm-filled garden is a healthy garden. If you like to fish, think of the garden as a storage area for fresh bait.

Frogs and toads. These eat bugs, too, and some frogs—notably the suction-padded tree frogs—sing for their supper. However, *Bufo marinus* toads, also called Amazon or Surinam toads—the ones that stare at your porch light and can grow big as soup bowls—emit a fluid poisonous to animals. Licking one can kill a puppy and make a grown dog sick. If you're a pet owner, best relocate or dispatch these toads.

Ant lions or doodlebugs. The larvae of the lacewing fly, a predator also considered a beneficial garden insect. The ant lion lives just below a conical depression it has dug in sandy soil, waiting for ants and other unlovable crawlies to fall in. The unwary travelers try to struggle back up the slippery slope, making a general ruckus. This attracts the attention of the owner, which grasps the victim in its pincers and pulls it into its lair.

Spiders. Useful creatures that package and devour insects gardeners are only too glad to be rid of. Just two South Florida spiders are poisonous—the brown recluse and black widow—and they're so rare you're unlikely to meet them.

Of dogs & toads

If your dog starts foaming at the mouth and hasn't been chewing on soap, chances are good he's been playing with a *Bufo* toad. Immediately and thoroughly rinse his mouth out with a hose. Rush a puppy or small dog to the vet. Observe a medium or large dog for additional foaming or signs of stomach upset, disorientation, or seizures. If you wash the poison out of a big dog's mouth right away, you've probably cured the problem. If you see strange symptoms, best take him to the vet, too.

Preying mantis. When you see a rare preying mantis in your garden, count yourself lucky. They eat just about everything you don't want.

Iguanas. They look like mega-lizards, but they're not plentiful and are very good at keeping out of sight. Having one in residence in your garden is a good thing. Iguanas have healthy appetites for bugs of all stripes and sizes, including the big roaches South Floridians call palmetto bugs.

Caterpillars turn into butterflies and moths. It's true that some are pests, but if you can find it in your heart to allow them some leaves, or can give them a few background bushes, the lowly caterpillars can reward you with sheer magic. Some gardeners go so far as to plant things especially to attract butterflies. Remember, too, that healthy caterpillars are good food for birds, whereas ones you've poisoned are not—and almost all gardeners enjoy having birds in their gardens.

Wasps and bees. Some wasps parasitize unwanted worms, stunning them and taking them back to their nests. Others lay their eggs inside their victims, preventing reproduction. Wasps and bees are famous pollinators, and the whole idea behind flowers.

measures, and use common-sense procedures.

Savvy gardeners water their lawns before dawn, when the grass is already wet with dew. Orchid growers dip their shears in fungicide before they divide a pot. Rose growers spray their plants weekly. Since a plant's outer sheath or bark is a natural barrier to fungus, if you treat an opening caused by pruning or an accident with fungicide right away, the risk of fungal infections is minimized. Citrus trees are especially vulnerable to opportunistic fungal invasions. A year after suffering an untreated gash, the tree may begin to decline from foot rot—and you may not even remember the reason. If left unchecked, a fungus can spread rapidly, causing living plants to decay just as surely as over-ripe peaches in a fruit bowl.

Fungus is the reason cuttings from succulent or sappy plants (cactus, plumeria, poinsettias, etc.) should be left to rest in the shade for a few days to a week to harden off before you plant them. Putting freshly cut, soft, green tissue into the ground—and then adding water—is an engraved invitation to the fungi always present in the soil. Small cuttings can be dipped in Rootone before potting. Rootone is a root-growth-promoting hormone that contains a fungicide.

Since most garden fungi are microscopic, fungal problems are usually diagnosed by the appearance of symptoms. In shrubs, fungi often reveal themselves in random unattractive blotches, spots, and irregular dying lesions on leaves and green tissues, or in stems that turn to mush.

In fruit trees, a fungus can cause young fruit to fall in disappointingly large quantities before it matures. Trouble is, too much or too little of certain food elements might cause similar symptoms. Deadly viral infections, toxic substances, and even some insects can, too.

Leaves turning brown from the tips back almost always indicates a root problem rather than a fungus. The roots have picked up something bad and pumped it up to the leaf tips. Fungus shows up more randomly across the leaves. Sickly-looking leaves or falling green fruit could indicate a nutritional problem. If you haven't used nutritional spray in a couple of years, maybe the plant is lacking some essential element. Since a good general nutritional spray contains a little bit of copper—a fungicide as well as a needed minor element —applying it may cure the problem, whatever it is, with one spray.

What kind of fungicide?

Each fungus has a particular preventative, but, since it would take a laboratory to define the exact fungus that's eating your plant, gardeners mostly rely on broad-spectrum fungicides, plus a few specific remedies for the usual suspects. If it's on a mango tree, for instance, it's probably anthracnose fungus; rose bushes most commonly suffer from black spot and powdery mildew.

Most fungicides are metallic. All are preventatives. The splotches you see on your plants will not go away. These leaves will die and fall off, or you can shear them off. The reason for applying fungicide is to prevent the rest of the plant from getting sick.

Contact fungicides work by coating the leaves and tissues of the plant with a metallic substance, such as copper. When a fungal spore lands on the metallic, it is killed. But there's a hitch: In one downpour, a contact fungicide may wash off in the rain, and its protection along with it. The use of a spreader-sticker can help it hang on a bit longer.

Systemic fungicides penetrate the plant's

tissues, so, once absorbed, are untroubled by the weather. This makes them superior for ornamental plants. But it's imperative to read and follow label directions. Manufacturers do not recommend systemics be used on edible plants within a certain time before harvesting.

Fungicides come on and go off the market so quickly that, if you think you may need one, it's best to be guided by someone up to date on the latest information. Local county agricultural agents can help, as can specialist plant societies or even a good nursery.

Fungicides are most effective when applied in liquid form, early in the morning or, second best, late in the afternoon, using as fine a spray as possible so the leaves are just coated. For lawns, move quickly, so the ground will not be drenched. And please remember to keep kids and pets off the grass until it dries.

Weeds

Weeds, as Harold likes to remind us, are only plants out of place. Looking out across a vivid meadow, you might not think of the wildflowers as weeds. But what if you find one abloom in your display of rare bromeliads? Consider a group of botanical collectors a few years back, overjoyed at their serendipitous discovery of rare epidendrum orchids growing on rooftops in a small tropical town in South America. The local residents thought these gringos were crazy to make such a fuss over the orchids, which were pests they'd been trying to get rid of for years.

Ultimately, it is the gardener who determines what is a weed and what is not, and this elevates weeding to the higher ranks of gardening operations. It can be enjoyable, too. Most nongardeners don't appreciate how therapeutic weeding can be, and have trouble fathoming how a gardener can contentedly devote hours to doing nothing but digging weeds (they don't realize the diggers are also secretly planning the next gardening project) until interrupted by someone announcing dinner, or driven indoors by mosquitoes or rain. And no one can deny a weed-free garden is a pleasure to behold. However, even gardeners who enjoy weeding, and admire the results, have their limits. Happily, weeds can be controlled in other ways.

Healthy grass and thickly planted ground covers can choke out weeds, and thriving shrubbery can shade many into oblivion. A three- or four-inch layer of mulch can help discourage weeds. Some gardeners claim lining the ground under the mulch with eight or ten layers of ordinary newspaper eliminates many weeds (nutrients, once dissolved soak through). In certain situations, though, most gardeners are grateful for a good garden herbicide. Manufacturers call these products "weed killers," but this can be misleading. Herbicides kill plants; the gardener decides which plants are weeds. Herbicides may look benign in their brightly colored jugs, but these chemicals are definite threats to valuable plants, and must be used with extreme caution. Harold compares herbicides to fire: beneficial and enjoyable in a fireplace, a cause for alarm on the living-room rug.

Gifts from the sky

If a volunteer (something you didn't plant) appears in your garden, don't be in a hurry to pull it out. Who knows? It might be an oak tree, flowering tree, Christmas palm, periwinkle, tomato plant, or any of a host of other flowers, vegetables, shrubs, and trees that are deposited daily in South Florida gardens, courtesy of wind and wayfaring birds. Once you've made a positive ID, you can usually dig it up and replant it in a better location.

Post-emergence herbicides

Post-emergence herbicides are designed to kill plants that are already up, growing, and driving you crazy. There are two basic types, selective and nonselective, and it's important to pay attention to which is which.

Selective herbicides. A selective herbicides "selects" and kills only certain kinds of plants, such as broad-leaf plants in a grassy environment. This type is widely used to kill weeds in lawns. Some of the broad leaf herbicides can be incompatible with South Florida lawn grasses. Like some Northerners, the chemicals mistake our grasses for broad-leaf plants. So the herbicide you select should say clearly on the label that it has been formulated for your kind of grass, or you may commit involuntary lawn-slaughter.

Granular weed-and-feed products can be especially insidious. Harold's neighbor was so satisfied with the rich green, weed-free lawn his weed-and-feed produced that he decided to use it every month (some monthly lawn-spray companies add weed-and-feeds, too). The herbicide gradually built up in the grass until, not dramatically, not spectacularly—just inevitably—the whole lawn turned brown and died. Since weed-and-feed type products are absorbed through the roots of all proximate plants, they may also affect shrubs and trees growing in or near the lawn. It might take years of consistent application to kill a large tree, but a little clump of marigolds may suddenly go down with a thud. For these reasons, weed-and-feed products deserve strict attention to application rates, timing, watering, and all their other directions.

Nonselective herbicides are designed to kill green plants. All green plants. One South

---

A weed to the wise

Post-emergence herbicides are best applied in a fine mist —never soak the ground—and always on a calm day so the spray doesn't blow onto other plants. If the chemical needs mixing before you spray, measure it precisely.

Incidentally, it's not a good idea to walk where you've sprayed; in ten days there may be brown footprints in your otherwise green lawn.

Florida gardener who failed to grasp this concept sprayed Round-up, an excellent nonselective herbicide, on his lawn. He knew what a weed was, and expected the Round-up to know, too. It did not. The grass browned and died. Used correctly, Round-up and its equally effective competitor, Kleen-up, are absorbed through the green tissues of plants and translocated to the roots, but leave the soil unaffected. They are known as systemic herbicides. They are used to eliminate weeds that pop up among patio stones and make mulch areas and pebble pathways unattractive. They may even be sprayed around mature trees (not young, green-barked trees) where you don't want grass to grow.

Soil sterilants are also nonselective herbicides, but so potent they can render the soil completely infertile for an extended period of time. As long as no feeder roots lurk nearby, soil sterilants could be used for keeping stone and mulch pathways weed-free. But these highly toxic chemicals are much more suited to commercial situations—in railroad yards and around warehouses. A soil sterilant will kill a tree stump, but it can also prevent anything else from growing in that spot for years.

Pre-emergence herbicides

As their name implies, pre-emergence herbicides are supposed to prevent seeds from

---

The invincible nutgrass

Nutgrass is not a grass, but a sedge. Individually it amounts to nothing more than a few long, slender blades emerging from the soil, but en masse can make your garden look as if it has grown a three-day beard.

Since it spreads via underground runners, it's undeterred by pre-emergence herbicides. Pulling one merely separates it from the rest of its rather large family, which takes this as a signal to call up the reserves. Nutgrass will not only poke through ten layers of newspaper topped with three inches of mulch, it will come up through asphalt. Unless you want to apply Round-up or Kleen-up to each sprout with an eyedropper, the only practical way to control nutgrass in a garden is to attack it with a hand-trowel and a vengeance. If it's in the lawn, mow it, forget it, and get back in your hammock.

germinating. This makes them useful in areas already landscaped You can sprinkle powder or spray liquid right over the mulch.

Brush killer

If you have a weed tree like Brazilian pepper or melaleuca, you can kill it by slashing the bark and painting on brush killer. The unwanted tree will absorb the chemical and die within in a couple of months. If you don't want to use chemicals, you can also kill the tree by chopping it down and assiduously knocking off all sprouts that appear, which will starve it to death (See "The essential leaf," page 103). This method can take somewhat longer.

Plant Collecting:
The Gardener's High

ollecting is an addiction suffered by gardeners everywhere in the world. In South Florida, where we're surrounded by such continuous seductive horticultural temptation, it's nearly impossible to just say no.

There are two basic kinds of collectors. One falls madly in love with one or two kinds of plants or flowers, and proceeds to encounter more and more difficulty resisting them. This is the well traveled road to orchid collecting, aroid collecting, hibiscus collecting, and even, if you have enough property at your disposal, collecting flowering trees. The specialist plant societies that flourish throughout South Florida are the collectors' support groups —only these support groups *encourage* the habit.

Collectors of the other sort are just plain fascinated by plants. All sorts of plants. They want one of everything. Harold Songdahl falls into this category. And over the years, as he shamelessly admits, he's had at least one of just about everything.

Most collections get started innocently enough. You purchase an orchid, or someone gives you a rose bush, and you're captivated.

You buy a book—which turns into a shelf full. Plants begin to accumulate. You get to talking to people with a similar interest, maybe join a plant society. And you're hooked. You may be induced to enter plants in shows. Given the choice between dinner at a fancy restaurant and the chance to purchase a rare specimen, which do you think you'll choose? And of course, your garden quietly begins to change, becoming a background for your prized plants. Some collectors evolve into hobbyists, learning to propagate or hybridize, becoming more and more expert. Some of the best have founded successful businesses.

It is not unusual for a collector of one kind of plant to branch out into related ones. Someone interested in orchids might well become fascinated with epiphytes of other kinds, such as bromeliads and ferns. Or they may go the other way, becoming absorbed in a single facet or sub-specialty, such as species orchids, miniature roses, or a single kind of fern. Whole books have been written about the staghorn fern, for instance, which comes in many varieties, with fronds ranging from a few inches to as much as ten feet long. Not all of them are easy to find. For some folks, tracking down their quarry becomes part of the fun.

It's easy to slip into collecting mode unawares. If you wake up one morning and find yourself surrounded by more specimen hibiscus bushes than are shown on your garden plan, it may be happening to you. Before your habit gets out of hand, there are a few things you can do to be sure your collection can be cared for and displayed as you want it to be.

144

Finding space

One advantage of living in South Florida is that you can establish permanent outdoor collections of things that would perish in climates just a few degrees cooler. Even so, the amount of outdoor space you have may physically limit the size or scope of your collections. Palms and other trees naturally require quite a bit of room. But so can collections of small plants like orchids if the collection grows large enough. Thirty orchid plants can be sheltered easily in the branches of a couple of trees, but unless you live in the woods, a few hundred almost certainly require a shade house. While most collections can be nicely incorporated into your landscape plan, some people prefer to keep their collections distinct from the rest of their gardens.

Plant societies

Roses, bromeliads, aroids, ferns, bamboo, rare fruit, flowering trees, African violets, begonias, cactus, bonsai, hibiscus, palms, and heliconias all have their societies. And there seem to be more orchid societies than orchids. Those fascinated by all sorts of tropical plants might join Fairchild, Flamingo, Selby, or other tropical gardens, or a general horticultural society, whose meetings are habitually attended by rare and interesting people who like to discover, grow, and talk about rare and interesting plants.

Even if you never go to a meeting, plant societies are worth joining. Their newsletters are usually crammed with topical and timely information pertinent to local South Florida conditions, and well worth the price of membership. Gardeners who actually attend the meetings, of course, can learn tremendous amounts from the experts who typically play featured roles there. Members also have access—through monthly raffle tables and inter-member plant sharing—to specimens not likely to be found elsewhere. And if elsewhere is where the plants are, plant societies often arrange collecting trips for its members. If you have the fare, you could hunt orchids in Brazil or rare species of bamboo in Thailand, and nobody would ever be bored by your conversation again.

As a bonus, most people in plant societies have garden-related interests apart from their specialties, so you can learn about other aspects of South Florida gardening, as well as the local geography and interesting places to visit, all with kindred gardening spirits. Joining a plant society is just about the fastest, most enjoyable way for newcomers to learn about gardening in South Florida—except, of course, reading *The Art of South Florida Gardening*. Here are some of the most popular of South Florida's collectible plants.

Aroids

Aroids are among the most tropical-looking of foliage plants. Scientifically, they are members of the *arum* family, whose plants are characterized by flowers—*inflorescences* to the horticulturally correct—consisting of a fleshy stem called a spadix surrounded by a flaring or hoodlike spathe. The largest known unbranched inflorescence on earth blooms on an aroid in the tropical rainforest. The titan arum (*Amorphophallus titanum*) is nine feet tall, with a trumpet-shaped spathe four feet high and three feet across. If you're downwind, you may be able to tell

Caladium

you're in its neighborhood before you see it by its strong scent of rotting fish. Arum means "odor" (think "aroma"). The titan arum is pollinated by tiny sweat bees, which seem to find the odor of rotting fish alluring.

Most South Florida garden aroids are odor-free (though not all: The fly-pollinated voodoo flower, *Sauramatum horsfieldii* grows here), which is fortunate, because aroids are everywhere. Elephant ears, whose edible version produces the malanga root, are aroids. So are dieffenbachias, spathiphyllums or peace lilies, anthuriums, and *Monstera deliciosa*. Caladiums are aroids. So are common philodendrons. And that's just the beginning. Collecting aroids is fun because of their diversity, even within each type. There are dozens of varieties and sizes of spathiphyllums, for instance. Anthuriums come in many sizes, their waxy, fake-looking heart-shaped spathes in colors ranging from red to pink to yellow to white to exotic patterns. Aglonaemas can be streaked with silver or splashed with gold. Caladium leaves come in various patterns and combinations of green, white, and arrestingly bright red. Alocasias can have prim valentine-shaped leaves or enormous pointed ones. Some elephant ears grow nine feet tall and have four-foot leaves. Others are ground covers just 12 inches high.

Elephant ears

Owing to their rainforest habitat, most aroids prefer filtered light, though some will take full sun for part of the day. They are excellent landscape plants, blending or contrasting well with other shrubs and plants, and growing thick and full, quickly filing in odd spaces. Most aroids also do well in atriums and in bright rooms indoors.

Aroids like to be kept moist. Some spathiphyllums will let you know in no uncertain terms when they're thirsty by wilting dramatically. Don't panic, just give them water, and in a few hours they'll perk right up.

Bamboo

Most bamboo is not native to the tropics. One of the largest bamboo collections in the country is in Washington, D.C., and many varieties grow in high Asian valleys among snow-covered mountains. But there are lots of tropical varieties that grow readily in South Florida, including Calcutta bamboo, from which the famous Calcutta fishing poles are made.

Bamboo is a grass. Some varieties are nearly as small as lawn grass, and can be used as ground covers. Others can grow 60 feet high and play the part of trees. Part of bamboo's appeal is its talent for graphic design. Bamboo stalks come in various shades of beige, yellow, orange, gold, black, or green; they can be smooth or textured; plain or striped or splattered with color —in short, ornamented in ways that have fascinated interior decorators and furniture makers through the centuries. Bamboo collectors are among the most passionate in South Florida, and have been known to jump in the car at a moment's notice and drive hundreds of miles to acquire a new specimen.

Bamboo in the landscape helps to create a peaceful sort of

tropical-Oriental atmosphere. Because even massive bamboos have a delicate appearance, they could take the place of a grove of trees—perhaps near a wall you don't wish to obscure completely. Some varieties do well in containers in bright areas indoors.

Like most grasses, bamboo spreads as it grows. Different varieties spread in different ways. A shoot of one kind may pop up less than an inch from the parent plant; others send runners eight or ten feet into the unknown before making their above-ground appearance—usually in the middle of a thorny bougainvillea, or worse, between the boards of your raised wooden deck. This kind of behavior might give you a headache if you're not prepared. But bamboo can be controlled. A sharp shovel or loppers can be used to cut off the corms or runners you see spreading beyond the limits you have set. Or a narrow (but deep) concrete footing could be poured around the plant, as a sort of subterranean wall. Smaller varieties can be confined to pots. And stands of bamboo can be thinned and sculpted just like any group of plants.

When bamboo sheds, it sheds a million little leaves. This is fine if the cascading leaves can filter through ground covers or into the grass. But pretty as it might look, try not to let anyone persuade you to plant bamboo near the pool.

Another trait peculiar to bamboo: Occasionally all the bamboos of a given clone in the world will, seemingly at the count of three, produce millions of seeds—and then die. This has proved tragic to pandas in China, but is only irritating to gardeners. No one has yet discovered a way to predict this strange bamboolian behavior.

Begonias

Begonias come in three types—the perky sun-loving fibrous-rooted begonias popular as annual bedding plants, the northern tuberous begonias with their gorgeous waxy flowers (these appear in the subtropics only as novelty plants), and the rhizomatous begonias, which are the South Florida collector's plants. Their foliage can range from dainty to immense, displaying colors and patterns so intricate and lovely it inspires artists and designers. These begonias typically bloom in arching sprays or form pendulums of flowers, usually in shades of red, pink, and white.

Begonia collecting is interesting not only because of the wide variety to be found, but because propagation is such fun. A stem in a glass of water or moist potting soil will easily sprout roots. Or you can half-bury a leaf in a container of good-quality potting soil, keep it moist, and watch new plantlets emerge from the margins of the leaf itself.

Begonias prefer liquid fertilizer, and, because they love shade, lend themselves well to leafy corners of the landscape, as well as to container gardens on porches and patios. Angel wing begonias are often seen in hanging baskets, lending a touch of romance to a subtopical terrace.

Bromeliads

Bromeliads are rarely seen in nature outside of the tropics. Though they are sometimes known as air plants, they do not live on air. Like orchids, most bromeliads are epiphytic, found clutching branches high in the rainforest trees (or hanging from them—Spanish moss is a rootless bromeliad), and nestling into rocks and boulders. You've probably eaten bromeliads: the ones called pineapples. Chances are, though, that there are many extraordinary bromeliads you've yet to meet, which is what inspires collectors. South Florida is home to many commercial growers and expert enthusiasts, including those involved in the various bromeliad societies, which means some of the finest bromeliads in the world can be found right here. Marie Selby Botanical Gardens in Sarasota is an international center for their study and display.

Bromeliads can range from thumbnail size to six or seven feet tall. Almost all share the same form: rosettes of stiff, concentric, recurved leaves forming a central cup. From this cup grows a flower—often a spectacular one, but sometimes one so tiny it cannot be seen. Bromeliads are grown as much for their colorful foliage as for their blooms.

The color of a bromeliad's leaves is a clue to its preferred habitat. Deeper greens need more shade; the more colorful ones can take more sun. Most prefer filtered light. Bromeliads may be attached to tree branches, affixed to rocks and

If you want to start a pineapple

If you already own a pineapple plant, by far the best way to propagate is to cut off and plant the ratoons—also called slips or suckers—that emerge from the base of the old plant. This is the way it's done on pineapple plantations.

You can also start your pineapple from the fruit. Don't cut off just the leafy top, but take a little of the meat as well. Plant in good soil, and have patience. Pineapple tops take longer to grow than ratoons.

Old bromeliads never die

Did you ever receive a bromeliad as a present? When it died, did you think it was finished and toss it out?

Next time, try tucking it into a shady, out of the way spot in the garden, and wait awhile. More than likely, young plants (pups) will emerge from around the mother plant.

Once the pups appear, you can cut the pups off the old plant (carefully; some of the pups might emerge right through the old leaves), and repot them. With normal bromeliad care, they should grow and bloom, and have pups of their own.

pieces of driftwood, steadied in pots and baskets filled with bark or stones, or clustered in a thick layer of organic mulch right on the ground. And bromeliads are excellent atrium plants.

Bromeliads take their nourishment from the water and organic substances that drop into their cups. In their natural habitats, you'd be surprised what bromeliads eat, and you might not want to know. This makes them very low-maintenance plants. Outdoors, you just keep their cups filled with water, and, if you wish, give them some liquid fertilizer once in a while. If you have a bromeliad indoors, hold back a bit on the water, or it may rot. (You'll find information about bromeliads and mosquitoes on page 76.)

Ferns

For most ferns, South Florida is a perfect home. Ferns do as well here as most fungi, and that's saying a lot. They love the high humidity and bountiful rainfall of summer. They do best in filtered light, but some don't mind the sun.

Wart fern

Ferns can be terrestrial (such as Boston, bird's nest, and fishtail ferns) or epiphytic (like the staghorn fern, resurrection fern, and the rabbit's foot fern with its furry rhizome). They reproduce from spores, not seeds, and never have flowers. If you see a bloom or fruit on a plant, you know it can't be a fern, though it may commonly be called one.

Like most collectible plants, ferns range from the petite to the gargantuan: a fern once found in South Miami had a frond 30 feet long. Tree ferns, which occur in nature in the islands south of Florida can grow 25 or 30 feet tall. Terrestrial ferns are usually very shallow rooted, and easy to start from a runner or a cutting, which makes them just right for planting at the base of a large tree. Ferns will drift and fill a space quite rapidly, which is nice at first, but they can become too much of a good thing. Fern collectors seem to be quite generous with their ferns. Moving very young plants with just a couple of emerging fronds is easiest, but you can transplant mature clumps, too—just trim off all but the new fronds, and plant the root mass. Keep it moist, and stand back.

Ferns can be effective worked into a landscape, massed around trees, hanging in baskets and pots, or affixed to the tree's bark itself. Some like to grow in the boots (the part that remains after a frond falls off) of date or cabbage palms. Many combine well with orchids and bromeliads. Ferns prefer liquid fertilizers or organics like Milorganite or fish emulsion. Dry chemical fertilizers can burn a fern.

Ferns aren't bothered by many pests, but some kinds can be totalled by snails and slugs. Be on the lookout.

Gingers and heliconias

Some people say "gingersandheliconias" as a single word, even though the plants belong to different families. Gingers and heliconias are often talked about and grown together because their jungly

---

Some native ferns

Boston fern, native to all of South Florida. It was first collected in South Florida by a New England botanist, and taken back to Boston, where it spread all over florists' greenhouses. From there it was shipped to England, where florists, apparently after a glance at the shipping labels, called it the "Boston" fern.

Long strap fern, native to central and South Florida and the Keys.

Maidenhair fern, native from Dade north to Volusia and Hernando Counties.

Resurrection fern, South Florida's most prolific epiphytic fern.

Heliconia

Staghorn stories

Staghorn ferns are those huge ball-shaped ferns whose projecting fronds are thought to resemble the racks of stags. A good-sized specimen can be six feet across—larger if it's grown on the trunk of a tree—and cost plenty.

• You can start your own staghorn fern from a single pup. With a sharp knife, cut a cone-shaped hole around the roundish shield from which the fertile frond projects, so you can take some of the root behind it. Don't worry. Soon new little ferns will appear all around the hole. It's important when you cut out the pup to remember which way is up.

Place the fern on a bed of wet sphagnum moss in a slat basket or on a piece of marine plywood into which you've hammered a circle of projecting nails. Hold the fern down on the moss and, using stretchy green plastic tape or monofilament fishing line, wrap it from one side of the basket to the other, or from nail to nail. The tape or line will be removed once the fern takes hold. Hang the board or basket so the fern projects from the side. As it grows, it will surround and engulf the board or basket. For a more permanent installation, you can tie the pup directly to a tree, securing it with green tape over moist sphagnum moss. Eventually, your fern will encircle the tree.

To hurry the process, half a dozen pups can be affixed around a tree-fern ball or around the tree, over a layer of sphagnum moss to retain moisture. Provide shade and water, and in a couple of years your pup will turn into a nice-sized fern.

• If you already have a staghorn so big it's about to break its chains, you can rehang it as follows: Drive a piece of galvanized

appearance and growth habits are so similar that many collectors of one have embraced the other.

Gingers and heliconias are upright plants with long, paddle-shaped, sometimes variegated leaves. They range in height from 18 inches to more than 12 feet tall. They are collected for their brilliant, sometimes fantastic inflorescences (the red and yellow lobster-claw heliconia is right out of a Rousseau

pipe or rod vertically through its center. At the bottom, thread on a T and two projecting pipes or rods for the fern to rest on. These will eventually disappear under fern fronds. At the top, attach an eye for the chain. If you hang the fern from a tree, be sure to protect the tree by running the chain through a piece of garden hose where it laps the limb.

• People often ask what the awful-looking brown stuff is on the undersides of their staghorn fronds. Is it fungus, they want to know? It is a colony of insects? It is none of the above. The brown stuff is the fern's reproductive spores, and means, says Harold, the plant is very sexy. If you want to try your hand at propagation, you can dust the mature spores onto a brick set in a pan of water in the shade. Keep the brick moist, but don't let it get rained on, and if you're lucky, a few new ferns might sprout.

• According to an old Florida wives' tale, staghorn ferns should be fed banana peels. Banana peels are full of potassium, which ferns enjoy—but they still need manure or other organic fertilizers. So if you don't relish the idea of banana peels rotting in the tops of your ferns, they won't feel deprived. If you really want to feed them banana peels, you can whirl them with some water in the food processor and serve them in liquid form.

painting) and their tropical-looking leaves, which are as marvelous in arrangements as the flowers.

In South Florida, we can grow many heliconia species straight from the jungle. Other varieties have been hybridized. University of Florida researchers are continually developing new gingers and heliconias for the cut-flower trade. The combination has produced a large and growing community of spectacular

Shellflower ginger

plants that produce pendulous or torchlike blooms in reds, oranges, blues, purples, and bright yellows. Perhaps the best known ginger is the *Alpinia speciosa*, or shellflower, with its tender pink pendant flower and green or variegated foliage three to eight feet tall. Other gingers come in yellow, red, orange, lavender, and coral. The fragrant white flowers of the mariposa or butterfly ginger are said, in Cuban lore, to bring good luck to the garden in which it grows.

Please don't eat the ginger

The family of gingers grown in South Florida includes commercial ginger—the kind whose root is used in cooking—but unfortunately this is not a very attractive plant. Collectors are interested in ornamental gingers, plants with attractive foliage and interesting flowers, but, alas, not much in the way of culinary appeal.

Like other plants with a rainforest heritage, gingers and heliconias are shallow-rooted, and therefore happiest in well-drained soil rich in organics and lavished with compost. They contribute to their own nutrition, dying back after blooming, their decomposing stalks enriching the soil. Replacement shoots soon sprout. If neatness counts in your garden, the dead stalks can be cut out, and the plants given balanced granular fertilizer monthly during their growing season.

Because of their habit of dying back after blooming, heliconias and gingers are sometimes considered background plants. Owing to their tropical natures, they can be quite sensitive to cold, and may die if not protected from freezes.

Many heliconias and gingers propagate by spreading, so don't be surprised if in a few years you find yourself lost in a flowering forest. You might have to be firm with them. Thin out, cut away, and give lots to friends.

Heliconia

Hibiscus

Hibiscus has always been a standard South Florida garden plant. Several dependable varieties have proven themselves fairly problem-free over the years, grown on their own roots in most kinds of soil: the bushy pink Anderson Crepe; the common red; the tall, weeping pink or white La France; the double red Old Reliable; the double yellow; and the Painted Lady (light pink centered with dark), which the American Hibiscus Society calls Miami Lady.

Collectors have expanded this roster to include many hundreds of varieties of grafted, hybridized hibiscus. Their color range is the rainbow, in every imaginable combination and intensity plus some the rainbow never heard of. They come in singles, doubles, and triple-deckers, in sizes from a few inches across to something big enough to be worn as a hat.

Young plants can be purchased at nurseries, but serious collectors often learn how to hybridize new varieties themselves. Results are so quickly apparent that propagating is easy and fun.

Hibiscus collections can easily be merged into the garden landscape, either by being co-mingled with other shrubs or showcased as specimens.

They make attractive standards (small trees). Harold was one of the first to begin the now fashionable practice of planting three or four tall young standards together in a big pot, and braiding their pliant trunks.

One day only

All you need to remember about hibiscus as a cut flower is this: With or without water, a hibiscus flower puts on a great show, but for only one day. Some hibiscus lovers report they can get a hibiscus centerpiece to last through dinner by refrigerating the blossoms for a few hours first.

Orchids

Orchids, arguably among the most magnificent of flowers, comprise the second largest family in the plant kingdom (only the grass family is larger), and are its most highly evolved members. Their sexual reproductive system is the most sophisticated of all plants. They include among their numbers some of the most beautiful—and some of the strangest-looking—flowers in the world. Harold says orchids are "exotic and erotic."

There are two basic types of orchid: sympodial, which have rhizomes from which emerge the leaves and flowers, and monopodial, which have erect stems or pseudobulbs that lengthen and thicken, producing the leaves and flowers. Not all orchids are tropical. Most are. Which means most will grow in South Florida.

Some orchids are terrestrial; they grow in the ground, like flame-orange *Epidendrum radicans*, and *phaius*, or nun's orchid. Before development encroached on the Everglades, Harold says, you could look across the marshes and see what looked like a field of pink and white wildflowers. It was thousands of *bletia*, terrestrial orchids with three-foot flower spikes.

Most orchids are epiphytic, found in nature growing in trees. The showiest epiphytic orchids are usually cattleya hybrids. Dendrobiums have sprays of blooms that can last for weeks. Other varieties include vandas, phalaenopsis (the charming moth orchid), oncidiums, and many more. Epiphytes are not parasites; they take no nourishment from their hosts, but merely hold on, gripping the bark with their strong roots. In nature, all the nourishment an orchid can ever expect comes from what mists down with the rain and blows in on the breeze in the tropical forests.

Some orchid flowers are large and headily

fragrant. Others are tiny, perfect miniatures, bursting forth in exuberant sprays. They come in every color and combination imaginable except black—and orchid hybridizers will probably never stop working on that. Growing and learning about orchids can be endlessly fascinating and supremely rewarding. In fact orchid growing is so popular in South Florida that more than 20 wholesalers and a few hundred retailers of plants, supplies, and equipment are kept pleasantly busy. Orchid societies are among the most active of South Florida plant societies, and there are numbers of amateur hobbyists who devote years to the leisurely pursuit of cultivating and hybridizing orchids. If you decide to collect orchids, you will have little difficulty finding all the plants, supplies, information, and encouragement you could possibly need.

If you intend to grow your orchids on tree branches (tied with stretchy green tape until their roots take hold; no wire, please), you should know their preferences, which can be surprisingly distinct. Their favorite trees seem to be citrus, mango, avocado, live oak, and bottlebrush trees, which offer nice, corrugated bark into which the orchids can dig their roots, healthful filtered light, and a rich environment of falling bugs and tree bits. Some palms are deemed suitable for habitation. Ficus trees make shade too dense for orchids, and, ironically, orchids almost invariably dislike Hong Kong orchid trees, whose environs they may find hostile and even deadly. Many collectors grow orchids in pots and baskets

A pair of native orchids

Cigar orchid (also called cowhorn or bee-swarm orchid), native from Lee County southward. Quite rare.

Florida butterfly orchid, the most common South Florida native orchid.

Florida's native orchids, like most native plants, are protected by law, and it is illegal to collect them from the wild without special permission. Selected clones are propagated, and are available to gardeners at specialist nurseries.

that can hang from the branches of their trees. This way the orchids can enjoy their preferred environment all through the year, yet be brought inside to be shown off when they bloom.

While orchids grow readily in South Florida, they have a few special needs. The medium in which they root, even though it provides no nourishment, should be chosen carefully—special bark chips, osmunda fiber (aerial fern roots), and various kinds of rock are favorites—for air circulation and good drainage. Orchid pots are also designed for drainage; in fact, the newest way to grow vanda orchids is in a slat basket without any medium at all—but very frequent watering. The fertilizer of choice is specially formulated orchid food, dissolved in water to be absorbed by the plants' highly porous leaves and roots. Orchids are fairly tolerant of cool temperatures outdoors, but can go down in a cold snap. Many orchid growers protect them with tenting or bring them indoors if the overnight temperatures are forecast to go below 40°F.

Roses

Many Northerners are amazed to discover that roses grow in South Florida. In fact, our rose bushes tend to grow much larger than the ones up north, and they bloom 12 months a year. Their flowers are just as ravishing, their fragrance just as alluring, and their thorns just as wicked as those of their cousins to the north. To a South Florida rose grower, they're among the most rewarding of plants, and well worth the attention they demand.

There are many kinds of roses: the large, specimen, long-stemmed hybrid teas and grandifloras; floribundas with their bouquet-on-a-stem blooming habit; dainty polyanthas; charming antique roses; climbers; and, the largest category of all, miniature roses. Many varieties from each group flourish here, but not all are able to withstand our hot summers or high humidity. Except for miniatures, which are usually grown on their own roots, the roses that do best in South Florida are grafted onto nematode-resistant and acclimatized rootstocks, the favorites being *Rosa fortuniana* and the old Cuban native, *Indica major*. They can be found at specialist rose nurseries and high-quality garden centers. Some catalog and inexpensive mass-market roses have been known to do well, too, until the nematodes do them in because they're on nonresistant roots.

Roses are ravishing in the landscape, and most grow well in containers, too, especially minis, many of which will grow and bloom without complaint on a sunny windowsill if that's all the space you have.

However, roses are definitely not something you can plant and forget. Fungus, notably black spot and powdery mildew, are year-round adversaries, and must be controlled with weekly sprayings of fungicide. In the dryness of winter and the heat of summer, during which a single bush can transpire as much as five gallons of water a day, roses need frequent, deep watering. Because they bloom all year, they are enthusiastic consumers of special rose fertilizer, and they aren't likely to turn down a few helpings of

Some almost-native roses

Over the years, a few kinds of roses have so successfully acclimatized themselves to the heat and rocky soils of South Florida they're considered nearly native. These are the rock roses or Key West roses. They are lovely in the landscape—not least because they're not very fussy when it comes to care.

The yellow variety is thornless and very fragrant; the small pink sweetheart rose is thick with thorns; the Seven Sisters rock rose bears clusters of smallish red roses.

All grow on their own roots, never need spraying (if a little black spot appears, the affected leaves can be snipped off), and when a bush gets too big for its space, you can prune it like any ordinary bush, and it'll come back thick and healthy.

Rock roses are rarely found at garden shops, so you might have to search one out at an old-fashioned mom-and-pop nursery, or have a friend give you a cutting.

other goodies, like alfalfa meal, Epsom salts, and Milorganite, at regular intervals, either.

If you give them what they need, indulge their cravings, and shower them with compliments, they will more than repay you with gorgeous flowers all year long—which is why rose collectors get hooked.

Indoor collections

Some plant collections must be kept indoors, in tightly controlled conditions. African violets, the most popular house plant in the world, are grown by plenty of South Floridians, and there is even an African violet society. But they are alien to our subtropical environment, so are rarely if ever found in the landscape.

There are also 14 varieties of native South Florida cactus (including tree cactus, prickly apple, and prickly pears found mostly in the hotter, drier areas of the Keys), and a few others that thrive in South Florida—notably the night-blooming cereus, spectacular specimens of which have been known to draw midnight gatherings of people to watch their buffet-plate-sized flowers open. But most exotic cacti would melt in the subtropical moisture. Serious cactus collections are kept mostly indoors.

The Weather Game

fficially, South Florida lies in the subtropics. But it is surrounded by the warm waters of the Gulf of Mexico, the Atlantic's Gulf Stream—the offshore current that flows up from the tropics, lapping close to our coastline—and the heat-retentive Lake Okeechobee and other large lakes. All this water tends to moderate even the infrequent and short-lived cold snaps that sometimes surprise Floridians from Tampa Bay and Cape Canaveral southward. And though we do, occasionally, experience a bit of frost (except Key West, the United States' only frost-free city), South Florida's climate remains nearly tropical for most of the year.

Gardening in this climatic paradise is a delight year-round—though in summer we force ourselves to postpone the pleasure until the cooler hours of early morning or evening —not least because of the exuberance with which plants grow, especially in rainy season.

This is not to say that tropical weather is without its challenges. In the rainy months from June to October, grass can grow as if extruded, while we watch through the downpours, hoping that when the rain finally stops long enough to mow the lawn, we'll still be able to

bully the mower through. In dry season, when an overnight low near freezing is forecast, we rush to bring our delicate orchids and bromeliads indoors, and to protect the vegetables we've babied from tender plantlings.

Normal hot and humid gardening conditions are routine for South Florida gardeners, whose equipment shelves contain (or should) large-brimmed hats, dark glasses, and plenty of sunscreen. But a few meteorological circumstances require special knowledge, supplies, and attention: drought, cold, and tropical storms.

Paradise dry

Logically, you wouldn't think the southern section of a subtropical peninsula composed mostly of swampland should ever be threatened by drought. And before the advent of the Army Corps of Engineers, it hardly ever was. Harold has met South Florida pioneers who knew the Miami River when it had rapids, and when artesian wells gushed fresh, sweet water up from the bottom of Biscayne Bay. Fishermen would stop their boats and dip up buckets of drinking water from the middle of the bay. At that time, Lake Okeechobee and the Everglades created a strong head of fresh water nearly as wide as the state, constantly replenishing South Florida's only source of fresh water, the underground reservoir called the Biscayne Aquifer.

But South Florida was far too attractive to remain pristine. Canals were dug to drain vast tracts of Everglades for farmland and, later, houses. This weakened the head of fresh water flowing toward Florida Bay, allowing heavier salt water to move inland beneath it. During dry spells, sea water would creep up canals and through the porous rock and sand, salting the aquifer to the point where it could be tasted in tap water. As more and more people moved in, to farm and live and landscape, and demand for water continued to grow, a succession of bureaucracies, starting with the South Florida Drainage District and culminating with the current South Florida Water Management District, attempted to control the supply. Dams were built at the mouths of the canals to keep salt water at bay. Pumps were installed to keep the canals from overflowing during periods of heavy rainfall. But none of the controls did anything to increase the supply or reduce the demand for water. Today in South Florida, fresh water is a precious resource.

Restricted water use is one of the rules of the gardening game. But water restrictions, far from being impossible to live with, are mostly codified common sense. Watering according to the rules of the South Florida Water Management District (no lawn irrigation between 9 A.M. and 5 P.M.) or those of your locality, usually meaning a few days a week before or after daylight hours, will give you a better looking lawn than if, left to your own devices, you watered every day at noon.

Back in the forties, before sprinkler systems, gardeners simply accepted the fact that South Florida had a dry season as well as a rainy season. In winter, lawns turned brown. In summer, they turned green again. Today it's beginning to become ecologically fashionable not to water during periods of drought. Even if your grass looks like shredded wheat for a few winter months, look around: So, probably, does everyone else's. Not watering is a way of showing respect for a limited resource. So is following the water restriction guidelines all through the year, even when rain is plentiful and the water table flush with sweet water. You've learned how not to waste water indoors; why waste it in the garden?

A limited water supply argues eloquently for xeriscaping. Those who have reduced lawn areas, used lots of drought-resistant plants, and kept their water-critical plants together and to a minimum hardly notice the dry season, and cruise through droughts without giving them a second thought. Those who haven't often decide to do so after a rainless winter.

A big chill

Every so often in winter, a great mass of frigid air from the Arctic, known locally as the Canadian Express, descends across the United States all the way to South Florida. Only Key West has continued to remain freeze- and frost-free. Luckily, the rest of South Florida usually warms up within a couple of days. But the temperature doesn't have to fall to 32 degrees for you to deploy your chill defenses. If the overnight temperature is forecast to fall below 40, it's time to get to work.

Here are the facts: 1) Because the coldest wind typically blows out of the north, on windy nights plants' northern exposures need the most protection. 2) Since frost forms mostly on plants out in the open, they should be shielded overhead. 3) Heat radiates upward from the earth; if you can contrive to retain some of it, the plants will stay warmer.

4) Low temperatures are moderated by the presence of water. That's why it's always a few degrees warmer at the beach, and why living on a canal, inlet, or lake can give you a margin of warmth on a nippy night.

Clouds are like a quilt on a cold night, reflecting radiated heat back down to the surface. On a cloudless night, we hope for wind, to blow the air around, helping to prevent the formation of frost. But if the night is cold and clear and still, the earth's radiated warmth rises straight up through the atmosphere and away, leaving the garden to shiver below.

Mulch ado about cold

Since one of mulch's functions is to insulate the ground, it makes sense to scrape it away from plants before a cold snap. This releases the heat from the soil, warming the foliage of the plants above.

You can protect movable plants by bringing them indoors or securing them in a shade house protected with sheets of plastic, on a porch or in a carport, or even under the eaves of the house or the branches of a large tree. This is especially important for tender plants like orchids and bromeliads. Many commercial growers, who take cold seriously, install heaters in their shade houses.

Most shrubs and trees can withstand a couple of nights of cold temperatures, but you can boost their self-protecting mechanisms by irrigating the day before a frosty night, so the water, warmed by the earth, will evaporate through the foliage at night. Even this tiny increase in temperature can make the difference between tolerably chilly and frostbitten.

Small trees can be protected with teepee frames covered in sheeting or plastic, or by a big cardboard box. A row of tomatoes or other tender vegetables can be protected in a sheet or plastic tent slung over a jury-rigged clothesline above. It's important not to let the fabric touch the plants, though. It will draw heat out of the leaves the way a tile floor sucks heat from your bare feet, and you'll find the leaves limp and withered by morning.

Many commercial growers, having discovered that crops can be kept warm under a coat of ice, irrigate continuously during a freeze. This can be effective if the system is correctly designed and used, but it requires some tricky technique. The plants must be continuously coated with water, requiring the use of a special cascade sprinkler. And the water must be kept going until the ice has completely melted. Even then, some plants break under the weight of the ice; others develop fungus problems from all the water. And if the freeze is particularly hard, continuous irrigation doesn't even work against cold damage. For private gardens, continuous irrigation is probably not a practical option.

A good freeze can do dramatic damage: crack a tree right down the middle or turn its top third completely brown or demolish a banana tree clean to the ground. With some plants, the damage is more subtle. Palms may appear scarcely affected, beyond maybe a few brownish fronds. But within a couple of years, if they start to decline and die, it may take a neighbor to remind you, as you're puzzling over the demise of your palm trees, about the big freeze two years before.

Although your first instinct after a freeze may be to cut off all the ugly brown branches on your trees and shrubs, it's best not to take freeze damage off quite so soon. This is because if it was an early freeze, another may be on its way—which could do additional damage to open tissue and newly sprouting shoots.

Also, it can take a few weeks for the true extent of the freeze damage to become apparent, and you can be more sure, then, of pruning back to good green tissue. On the other hand, if it's a banana that's been leveled, sure, whack it off. No sense leaving any soft-tissued plant to lie around liquefying in the garden. New shoots that appear will have to take their chances.

Some plants can actually appear to improve as the result of a bracing, wood-chilling freeze. The outer tips of *Euphorbia punicea*, a smallish tree with bright red flowers, may appear to have melted after a freeze; if you control your urge to trim them, these tips will fall off in a sort of natural pruning process, and the tree will grow even bushier. Some elephant ears will seem to dissolve completely —only to triple their numbers. Ti (pronounced tee) and corn plants, having died back, will often produce six to eight shoots for the price of one. Amaryllis tends to cluster, while the Eucharist or Amazon lily has been known to produce dozens of flowers during the blooming season following a freeze. And citrus does sweeten in the cold.

Gardeners who prefer not to deal with freeze damage can plant things that are more hardy. Gardenias, podocarpus, arboricolas, pittosporum, and most native plants will find the cold nights invigorating. Nourishment is also a factor. A plant that goes into the cooler months well nourished stands a far better chance of weathering the cold than one suffering from malnutrition.

Hurricane watch

Tropical storms—the most violent of which are hurricanes—can tear your garden to shreds, blow it away, wash it out, poison it with salt water, or all of the above. But while it may look like a war zone the morning after, have faith: Your garden will rise again.

The winds in the weakest hurricane blow 74 miles per hour, more than fast enough to topple a tree, kick your lawn furniture across the street, or turn a screen enclosure into scraps of mesh and metal. If it's a wet enough storm, the soaked ground, especially clay or sand, can release its grip on roots, making trees even more vulnerable to the wind. Floods are common in hurricanes. Contaminated water is routine. Electricity and telephone service can be out for weeks afterward. The idea of a hurricane may be thrilling, but, as everyone knows who endured the terror of 1992's Hurricane Andrew, the real thing is deadly serious.

The best long-term strategy you can adopt to counter the threat of a hurricane is to keep your plants and trees healthy year-round. For a sickly or declining tree, a tropical storm can be the *coup de grâce*. Keeping plants healthy means watering deeply to encourage strong, tenacious root systems; giving them ample nourishment throughout the year; and keeping them well shaped, with an open canopy that presents the least resistance to a relentless wind. Even well-fed and well-groomed trees aren't guaranteed to withstand very strong winds and heavy rains. But at least you'll give them a fighting chance.

Smart gardeners don't wait for a hurricane warning to have their trees trimmed. The tree companies will be rushed, you'll get a bad job, and the dump will refuse branches if the hurricane is imminent. The last thing you want is a pile of cut up branches in front of your house, each of which can become a missile in the arsenal of an angry storm. But if you don't have your trees trimmed, nature

How to right a fallen tree

Trees knocked over by the wind (or overzealous post-storm bulldozers) can be saved if you act fast. Here's how:

- Reduce the canopy by pruning off at least a third—and as much as half—the branches. This conserves moisture in the tissue of the tree, and reduces its weight. Since the tree must produce new feeder roots before it can absorb nutrients for food, it won't need all its leaves for a while anyway.

- Cut off all broken roots.

- Clear out the rocks, branches, and other foreign material that have found their way into the hole.

- Prop up the tree, shoveling and watering the soil back around the roots and into the hole.

- Secure with heavy-duty stakes and wires. Use materials stout enough to be left for a year.

- Some people recommend spraying all the damaged tissue with a broad-spectrum fungicide as a preventative. The tree has been through enough, they reckon; it doesn't need a fungal attack, too.

- Water and feed as if it were a newly planted tree.

It's best for the tree to be stood immediately, because the sun can damage previously unexposed trunk and roots. If it will be a few days before you can get to the tree, cover the trunk and roots with a blanket or a sheet of burlap, shade them with palm fronds, or white-wash the trunk with cheap white latex paint (it will flake off after a while). Otherwise, without a canopy to shade the trunk and branches, the tree can die from sun scald.

will eventually do it for you, and she does a terrible job. Hurricanes commonly leave neighborhood lawns and roads completely blocked by fallen trees and massive branches. Young men with pickup trucks and chain saws can make big money chopping up fallen trees and piling them on the swale—cash only, of course. And unless you take your own limbs to the local dump (or, as it's now called, the transfer station), that pile can wait many months for the county to get around to it. Having your trees properly trimmed on a regular basis will give you one less thing to worry about when the storm warnings sound.

If a hurricane is expected, after you've rechecked your family's stock of hurricane supplies, and after you've secured the storm shutters and roof ventilators, it's time to work on the garden.

Take everything you can indoors. Don't expect your shade house to offer any protection whatever to the plants or equipment inside. After the storm, you'll be lucky if the shade house is still there. If some potted plants are too large to bring in, lay them on their sides in the most sheltered corner of your yard. Tie garden furniture to the fence.

Don't bother trying to protect shrubs. The ones still there after the storm will have sustained

---

Salt-tolerant plants for seaside gardens

Natives

Cocoplum. Native as far north as Stuart and Sarasota. Grows well on dunes.

Inkberry. Native to the Keys. Impervious to salt spray.

Necklace pod. From the Keys to Palm Beach and Fort Myers.

Sea lavender. Native to South Florida. Plentiful in Palm Beach area.

Wax myrtle. Native throughout Florida.

Wild coffee. South Florida and the Keys. Not the drinking kind.

Coontie. Throughout Florida.

Spanish bayonet. Throughout Florida.

Other shrubs and ground covers

Wedelia, periwinkle, purple queen, crown of thorns, mondo grass, kalanchoe, blue daze, sprengeri, beach daisies, oleander, pittosporum, *Carissa grandiflora*, scavola, viburnum, ligustrum, sea grape.

Vines

Confederate jasmine, Mexican flame vine.

wind damage, but this is usually not a lasting problem, especially if they're healthy to begin with.

Be sure you have the tools you'll need to clean up after the storm has passed: Lengths of rope and two-by-fours to stand a fallen tree. Rebar and a big hammer. Sharp saws and pruners. Buckets for bailing or for dipping water out of a pool. When there's no running water, this can save your favorite shrubs. You may also want to invest in a chain saw—or go partners on one with a neighbor. Don't forget the gasoline. Lawn-care people often disappear after major storms—and grass can come back with a vengeance after the heavy rains—so be prepared to cut your own grass.

A hurricane storm surge, in which ocean water can intrude for miles inland, can make garden soil salty and toxic to many plants. Even torrents of rain water are usually insufficient to purge the salt that may have encroached in a storm surge, since the rain water may have been scooped up from the sea by the storm, and be nearly as salty as the ocean.

After a storm, therefore, it's prudent to hose down all your plants thoroughly with fresh water as soon as you can. Unless a plant is salt-tolerant, salt water can kill it.

Terrible incursions of sea water can be caused by some storms. In past hurricanes, Key Biscayne has been known to go nearly completely under, and grunts and snappers have been seen flipping around on front lawns along Miami's Brickell Avenue. Plant roots can't help but absorb all the salt water surging through the ground. Because the areas near the shores are always hardest hit, good landscape strategy for waterfront property is to use a high proportion of coconut palm trees and other salt-tolerant plants.

You'll have plenty of pruning to do after a hurricane. It's important to a good job, cutting into healthy green material below the point of damage, and reshaping the tree or shrub as best you can. After a few months, when the new leaves and branches appear, you can do another trim.

Be prepared for everything to look as if a hurricane has hit it for at least several weeks. Then, miraculously, almost everything in the yard will start coming back again. This can be a powerful spirit lifter, especially to people living in tents, trailers, and blown-out houses without electricity or telephones. Of course, weeds, which have no sense of decency, also come back, in droves. Try not to feel pressured by all that's crying out to be fixed and straightened and pruned and fed out in the garden. Every family in the neighborhood is trying to cope with its own version of storm trauma, including damaged houses, trailer-living, difficulties with insurance companies and contractors, and all the other emotional upsets that come in the wake of a big storm. The yard is going to get ahead of you, and it's not the end of the world. Taking it section by section, project by project, interspersed among the hundreds of other things that need to be tended to, you'll eventually restore the garden to its former magnificence.

What Andrew taught us

Besides interrupting the writing of this book, Hurricane Andrew, which blasted across south Dade County in the pre-dawn hours of August 24, 1992, taught South Florida gardeners some valuable lessons. Andrew was a Category 4 hurricane, meaning its sustained winds were more than 131 miles per hour, and many folks living in its path can attest to terrifying gusts considerably stronger than that. All the predictions and guidance Harold had given before Andrew's visit were validated in three dimensions and living color, with the exception of the saltwater danger, since Andrew was a relatively dry and fast-moving storm, and whatever saltwater it deposited was subsequently rinsed away by several weeks of rainy weather.

Nevertheless, even Harold, who lived through what seemed to him to be a hurricane per season as he was growing up, acknowledged that those were rain squalls compared to Andrew, which he experienced at close range, his house being located in the path of the storm's vicious northern eye wall. After the storm, he made some personal observations, and distilled them into the following additional hurricane advice:

Before the storm

• If you can afford a chain saw, and know how to use it, buy one. After the storm, your neighbor will be using his. Be sure to store enough fuel and a spare chain.

• Have some rebar of varying lengths on hand for propping up small trees fast. A few lengths of two-by-fours and sturdy line will come in handy for larger trees. A bundle of tomato stakes and green garden tape is good for small shrubs.

After the storm

• Shingles being hurled by 140-mile-an-hour winds can pierce trees, and even concrete walls, like daggers. A chain saw can turn hidden imbedded shingles into flying shrapnel. So be careful out there.

• Apart from cutting up branches and hauling them to the curb, you'll probably be so fully occupied with home repairs that you won't have much time for righting trees or doing other garden repairs for a while after a good-sized storm. But, since lying on its side in the blazing summer sun can kill even a large tree, if you plan to try to save it, at least cover it with a tarp or a sheet while it's waiting.

• You won't be able to save everything, so be prepared to prioritize. If there's something you really don't want to lose, do all you can to save it. The less important things can be replaced.

• Without the protection of big trees, some shade-loving plants—and plant collections—can suffer. If you want to save them, it's important to get some shade cloth up as quickly as possible. Jury-rig at first, but try to do a more permanent job as soon as you can get around to it. More than three years after Andrew there was still not much shade in south Dade.

• You may need to relandscape after a big storm, since most of the trees may have blown down. On Harold's block, the only tree left on the swale in Andrew's wake was a golden showers which presented little resistance to the wind, since its idiosyncratic owner had hatracked it annually, usually by moonlight, to little more than a trunk. After Andrew, the owner moved away, and the tree was free to flourish at last. Treat your new landscaping as a fresh project, with a new vision from which to plan, and even make improvements. You can use the opportunity to plant trees where you need shade, to plant intelligently, and to plant things you really want— and that might have a chance of surviving next time.

• Beware of being in such a rush to put in new trees that you accept inferior specimens or ones that might have a hard time in South Florida. Even trees that grow superbly here, like live oak trees, don't generally do as well here unless they were born and raised somewhere in our area. And if you want a live oak, insist on a live oak. Laurel oaks and other varieties are not good substitutes.

• Don't be in a big hurry to take out plants that appear to be dead. Leave them awhile and see what happens. After Andrew, many plants that looked as if they'd never sprout again surprised gardeners by coming back as green and full as ever. Some good self-repairers were banana trees, selloums, aralia, bougainvillea, and gardenia. Live oaks, mahogany trees, and palms also seemed to do especially well.

• Have patience. After a hurricane, a thousand things will need to be done in every part of the garden. Gradually, one area or project at a time, you'll bring it all back to normal. Be prepared for this to take some time, and for things to get way ahead of you for a while. Take what comfort you can in knowing that all your neighbors, and those living in communities for miles around, are in the same situation.

The comeback kids

Of the Florida Forestry Division's recommended shade and flowering trees to plant in South Florida, Harold likes the following for hurricane resistance or quick post-storm recovery:

Green trees

Natives: black ironwood, white stopper, soapberry, blolly, Jamaica caper, mastic, silver buttonwood (in shore areas), green buttonwood, Spanish stopper, willow bustic, dahoon holly, paradise tree, pigeon plum, pitch apple, lysiloma, gumbo limbo, red maple, West Indian mahogany, live oak.

Nonnatives: pandanus, weeping podocarpus, yew podocarpus.

Flowering trees

Geiger (native, but cold-sensitive), cattleya guava, coral bean, dwarf poinciana, frangipani, parkinsonia, lignum vitae, sweet acacia, white geiger, yellow elder, yellow tabebuia, bottle brush, buttercup, golden shower, Hong Kong orchid tree, pink tabebuia, queen crape myrtle, copperpod, silk floss, jacaranda, royal poinciana.

Note: Most palms are hurricane-resistant, and many fruit trees recover relatively quickly after a storm.

Harold's Laws of the Garden

Truths gleaned over many years of gardening in South Florida

A lost garden tool will reappear within 24 hours after it has been replaced.

If you feel like mowing the lawn, it will rain. If you want to get out of mowing, it will be 72° and partly cloudy.

You can't outsmart Mother Nature.

The chances of your house's being infested with termites are directly proportional to the value of the shrubs you've planted too close to the house to clear the fumigation tent.

The day after you plant the shrubs you bought triumphantly on sale, you'll see them somewhere else even cheaper.

Simultaneously with pulling the trigger of the weed-killer spray bottle, you'll realize you aren't aiming at a weed.

When you have pulled the hose to nearly its full length, it will kink at the other end.

If you need 20 plants, 19 will fit in your station wagon.

No plant is ugly; some just have more character than others.

The label on the insecticide can is designed to slowly self-destruct so that it disintegrates completely just before you need to read it.

(Corollary: The more toxic the insecticide, the smaller the print on its instruction label.)

Moments after your automatic sprinklers turn on, the heavens will open.

Your kids will resolutely refuse to pull weeds in your garden, but will happily pull them next door.

A puppy given the run of the yard will select the most expensive young rare fruit tree to dig up.

If you painstakingly explain to your neighbor why something he has in mind to try won't work, and he goes ahead and does it anyway, it will work.

The place you've selected to plant a tree will turn out to be in the center of your yard's largest submerged rock.

Your mower will contain sufficient gas to cut seven eighths of the lawn.

The people next door will buy an outdoor barbecue grill as you remove the last plant in your ten-foot hedge.

There is always one more weed.

Water Ways

I n South Florida, nature usually supplies enough water, in the form of rain, to maintain native, acclimatized, and low-maintenance exotic plants year-round. Grass, new plantings, and all plants that require more water than rain provides may depend, from time to time, on you.

Some plants, like the spider plant and sprengeri, have learned to coast through dry spells by storing water in underground tubers. Others greedily drink all they can get and, it seems, immediately ask for more. Grass is gratefully green in summer, but would hibernate in winter if you didn't keep it awake with irrigation. Plants in quick-draining sandy or rocky soil need more water than plants in marl, and potted plants require more frequent watering than plants in the ground. Here's how to keep all your plants well quenched.

A good hosing

The simplest and least expensive way to water a garden is to stand with a watering hose in one hand, morning or evening, a couple of days a week. Holding a beer in the other hand is optional. Hose watering is efficient, since you water only as long as is needed, and can aim the stream where it will do the most good, drenching the soil without wetting leaves or washing down the driveway. If you want to get fancy, you can purchase a wardrobe of watering gadgets and nozzles for your hose—a fan-shaped one for a gentle rainlike spray, perhaps, or a bubbler for on-the-ground watering, or one with a choice of sprays from fine to coarse to a shooting stream. Many gardeners wouldn't trade their hoses for anything, nor the pleasant moments they spend watering their gardens. Standing or sitting there with a hose does require a certain investment in time, however.

Add a sprinkler

It's a bit much to expect even dedicated hose enthusiasts to hose-water their lawns. For this purpose, sprinkler heads can be attached to the end of the hose. There are oscillating sprinklers, fountain types, whiz heads for fast volume, or the impact sprinkler that makes lazy circles as it sends romantic-sounding streams of water over the grass. Timing your lawn sprinkler to go on and off is a simple matter of checking your watch, going outside, and rotating a valve counterclockwise and clockwise, respectively.

Sprinkling on command

For those who wish to water the whole property at once, the sprinkler system was developed. This consists of an underground system of PVC piping attached to a water supply and perhaps an automatic timer, with strategically placed sprinkler heads that spray water from high around the perimeters of the yard, or pop up from the ground. The advantage of an automated system is that it doesn't require much attention (until something breaks). A disadvantage is that a lot of the water applied by the sprinklers may be lost through evaporation before it has a chance to penetrate to the grass roots. Also, up to recently, sprinkler timers couldn't tell when it was already raining, giving rise to lawns being merrily sprinkled during raging thunderstorms. These days, in many communities, rain-sensing sprinklers are mandatory.

A real drip

An improvement for garden watering was the invention of the drip system, promoted by xeriscapers because water goes nowhere but into the soil, at the point you direct it, at a slow, steady pace that keeps soil uniformly moist, through a system of tiny tubes and emitters. Drip systems are easy to design yourself from materials and kits at the local garden supply depot. They're excellent for planted areas and potted plants, but fairly useless for lawns.

All that wilts does not need water

Though in normal circumstances wilted plants are crying out for water, sometimes they're sending a different message. After a day or two of nonstop rain, for instance, the sudden appearance of a hot afternoon sun can shock a plant grown used to solid overcast. Heat stress can produce wilting. But after all that rain, the last thing your plant needs is additional water. Shade it if you can, or, if it's a robust plant, let it be. It will revive when the sun goes down.

Turn it off!

Over-watering wastes water and can harm plants. In containers, more plants die from too much water than from too little. Too much water can waterlog roots and encourage fungus and rot. And soggy soil can deprive roots of oxygen, which can turn leaves yellow.

Plants do best in uniformly moist—not wet—soil, which is why sensible watering and good drainage are so important.

The hose that soaks

In an ingenious expansion of the drip idea, porous hoses made of recycled car tires—an ecological plus—are arranged in trenches under the lawn, or just beneath the mulch in planting beds. When the water is turned on (just a smidgen is enough), it slowly, steadily oozes through the soaker hose and directly into the ground. Soaker hose systems can be put together and installed yourself, or there are companies you can hire to do it for you.

Xeriscaping, South Florida–style

"Xeri" is from the Greek word xeros, meaning "dry." Originally dreamed up in desert country, where people got tired of trucking in sod and using tons of water just to maintain the illusion of the suburbs, the term xeriscape (say "zeri-scape") meant a landscape that did not require more water than was provided by nature. Desert gardens became arrangements of rocks, sand, cacti, succulents, and perhaps a few drought-tolerant native trees and shrubs. A garden of desert cacti and succulents— which come in every color and an amazing variety—can be stunningly attractive.

In South Florida, it is also possible to achieve a garden of rocks and succulents and local cacti. But here the meaning of xeriscaping has been relaxed and expanded somewhat, to bring it more into harmony with the subtropical richness that surrounds us. Here, xeriscaping means strategic planting and intelligent water management. The attraction of xeriscapes is that they really do make sense, ecologically and economically.

The foundation of a good South Florida xeriscape is drought-resistant trees and shrubs mingled with appropriate native plants. Natives must be chosen carefully, though. Some like their natural habitat so much they have trouble making the transition into a garden setting.

South Florida xeriscapes may include some lawn, but perhaps not as much as traditional landscapes. These landscapes may include plants that need moderate and sometimes even large amounts of water. What makes them xeriscapes is that the plants are arranged in the garden according to their water requirements. They're then given soil amendments and are properly mulched, so that, after they are established, their needs can be attended to without wasted time, effort, funds—or water.

Water watchers

Plants that wilt when dry (coleus, spathiphyllum, impatiens) can be planted among other kinds, as indicators that the whole area needs water.

Plants with Personality

n the most well-orchestrated gardens, some plants sing. One or another quirk or characteristic sets them apart from the rest. One might be distinguished by an unusual coloration or silhouette. Another may have an intriguing growth habit or reproductive method. Though not always rare—most of the plants mentioned in this chapter can be easily found—and not necessarily things you'd think of collecting (though of course collectible plants have plenty of personality), plants with personality can add unexpected spice to a landscape.

There are many, many plants with personality. A source of continuing amazement to South Florida gardeners is the number and variety of endlessly fascinating plants that thrive here. And it seems more and more are being imported, tested, and put on the South Florida market as they are discovered in similar habitats around the world.

Like many plant enthusiasts, Harold is always on the lookout for new and interesting arrivals. The plants described on the following pages are some of his long-standing favorites. No description is as good as a look, though, so if these short profiles and simple illustrations whet your interest, the next step is to go and see these personality plants at your favorite nursery or garden store.

Agave

The common name of agave (pronounced a-*ga*-vay) is century plant—presumably because of the legend that it takes a hundred years to bloom. This is not quite true, though it can sometimes seem like a hundred years. Agave is a succulent plant grown in Mexico for its fibers, which are made into rope, and, perhaps more interesting to some, its juice, which is made into tequila. In South Florida, we grow agave for its visual drama. Some varieties are like giant round pincushions with spiny points; others contort their leaves, which can grow to eight feet long, in spirited twists and convolutions. Their subtle colors—greens, grays, and variegated—make attractive counterpoints in a landscape.

The agave's flower spike, when at long last it appears from the center of the plant, is held aloft by a stalk that may in some varieties rise many feet in the air. There it sends out lateral arms covered with flowers, usually cream-colored, which, when pollinated, develop into delightful little plants right up there in the sky. When the mother plant weakens and dies, the stalk collapses, scattering all the new plants over the ground where, in nature, they do their best to take root. In your garden, you can pop them off and pot them up.

Agave likes soil on the dry side, and is generally not very demanding, which makes it doubly nice to have around.

Bird of paradise

Bird of paradise (*Strelitzia reginae*) is among the most tropical of flowers. Its royal blue and orange blooms, like feathers on the fantastic head of some mythical jungle bird, are among the most eye-catching in the garden, and are impressive in cut-flower arrangements. The plant itself is a clump of spear-shaped leaves four or five feet tall. It can, over the years, turn into quite a large clump.

Its pale-plumed cousin, the white bird of paradise (*Strelitzia nicolai*), bears its equally striking cream-and-blue flowers amid fans of large, tropical-looking paddle-shaped leaves. Many people grow the white bird just for its leaves. Though the plant can reach as high as 20 feet at maturity, it may be planted closer to buildings than similar-sized trees.

Both kinds of birds are related to the banana, and, like bananas, need rich, peaty, acidic soil, adequate moisture, and plenty to eat, in small portions at frequent intervals. They bloom best in sun, though the plants themselves tolerate half shade. Bird of paradise clumps can be divided if necessary. To keep the white bird within bounds, you can cut away the small shoots that hatch at its feet.

Brunfelsia

Brunfelsia is a stunning flowering shrub that, in some varieties, produces small, flat-petaled violet flowers that gradually fade to lavender and white, giving the shrub the appearance of blooming in three colors at once. It is this personality quirk that inspired its nickname, "yesterday, today, and tomorrow."

The variety that does best in South

Florida, however, *Brunfelsia grandiflora grandiflora*, blooms in lavender and fades to white. So Harold affectionately refers to it as "yesterday, today, and no tomorrow."

Brunfelsia will develop into a naturally rounded shrub that can grow as high as ten feet or so, but of course can be kept lower. It can also be shaped into an eye-catching multitrunked tree. It prefers full sun, and is a ravenous eater that will gobble up a monthly serving of granular fertilizer, and may appreciate some liquid fertilizer in between.

Brunfelsia blooms only on new wood. This means that, for the best bloom production, after its fall and winter blooming period is over, you should pinch out the growing point of each stem at regular intervals, to encourage branching and, as a result, even more flowers the following year.

Cycads

As a species, cycads are among the oldest plants on earth, having survived virtually unchanged since before the dinosaurs. Probably the best known cycads are the zamias (coontie, cardboard zamia) and the various sagos, commonly and inaccurately called sago palms. Cycads are not palms, but are similar in appearance and are sometimes mistaken for them. Sagos are characterized by circular tiers of dense green fronds that turn into brown grass skirts as the plant grows. Most make eye-catching specimen plants. And cycads require little water.

Cycads reproduce sexually. A cone-bearing cycad is female. Harold discovered as a kid playing soldier that the grenade-shaped zamia cones, if tossed at the right moment of ripeness, explode on impact, unleashing their shrapnel of scarlet seeds.

Eucharist lily

The Eucharist lily (*Eucharis amazonica*), also called the Amazon lily, is the daffodil of the south, adding a similar cheerful charm to shady areas. Grown from a bulb (it's related to the amaryllis), it has broad and arching green leaves that make handsome foliage all year. The flower is white and pale green and is composed of a ring of petals surrounding a central trumpet that makes it look something like a jonquil. Eucharist lilies tend to bow their heads like bells; if you want them to show their trumpet centers you can prop them up with bamboo orchid stakes. When mature, they bloom several times a year.

Making new plants is easy. When the original pot gets crowded, just dump out the bulbs, separate, and replant them in new containers. Harold likes the effect of planting a trio of bulbs (large, medium, and small) in an eight-inch pot.

Firecracker plant

The firecracker's Latin name is *Russelia equisetiformis*—and its flowing, green sprays of foliage could resemble something "shaped like a horse's tail." The common name, firecracker, was inspired by its clusters of small, tubular, flame-red flowers. Firecracker plants are used as ground covers. They're good-sized plants that can cover a lot of ground.

They can imitate a fountain splashing from a big container, or cascade from a broad balcony planter. They need plenty of sun to bloom.

Dracaena marginata

These elegant dracaenas, also called dragon plants, with their slender, crimson-edged leaves and slim curving branches, were once so valuable and rare that good specimens used to be swiped right out of front yards. They were in such demand by interior designers that specialist growers used to devote themselves exclusively to "sculpting" them. Rows of tall plants standing shoulder to shoulder would be weighed down with half-full water jugs, bricks, auto parts, and other heavy bits of junk, encouraging the branches into interesting bends and curves—and giving the nurseries the appearance of junkyards. Now sufficiently plentiful not to be

How to train a dragon

You can easily train a *Dracaena marginata*, or dragon plant, into interesting bends and twists, producing a specimen referred to in horticultural circles as having "character."

Tie an empty plastic jug within a foot or so of the end of each branch you'd like to sculpt, and slowly pour water into the jugs until the branches begin to bend.

Add water a little at a time, in stages a couple of weeks apart so the branches don't break from too much sudden weight. Once the branches bend lower than horizontal, their tips will begin heading skyward again, and additional shoots will usually erupt at the bends.

You can also sculpt a marginata by amputating some of its branches at various heights. Each will produce two to five new branches.

To propagate the ends you've cut off, just root them in a pot of moist soil. Don't keep it too wet, or the cuttings may rot. Harold likes to root a single large cane with several interesting branches (for instant character), or three cuttings of staggered lengths, perhaps two, four, and six feet tall, together in a simple clay pot. When the new plants are ready to be displayed indoors, their pots can be slipped into cachepots or jardinières.

nicked from under your nose, *Dracaena marginata* is still a very desirable plant, and a nicely trained one can look as striking as a work of art spotlit in front of a bare wall.

Members of the lily family, marginatas can grow to 30 feet tall and develop trunks three feet across, though most people keep them trimmed substantially smaller. Dracaenas require very little care or water. This suits them for growing in containers and, in good light, indoors. They're such energetic growers that if necessary they can be sawn off at ground level—and will come back good as new. They drop a lot of ribbony leaves, however, so it's not a bad idea to surround them with ferns or other large-leafed plants as screens or filters.

Euphorbias

Euphorbias belong to a large family of plants whose looks can vary amazingly, but which share at least one common characteristic—a milky, staining sap that can irritate the skin. Some euphorbias are naturally multiple-trunked and can be grown as shrubs or small trees (the red-flowered *Euphorbia punicea* and *Jatropha integerrima*); others are low shrubs (the prickly crown of thorns, the colorful croton). Some euphorbias are easily mistaken for cacti. The brain cactus is actually a candelabra euphorbia hosting a benign resident virus that curls its stems; the pencil cactus is also a euphorbia. Probably the best known euphorbia around the world is the poinsettia (*Euphorbia pulcherrima*).

Euphorbia
punicea

Newcomers, accustomed to seeing poinsettias only in foil-covered pots during the holiday season back home, are often charmed to find them blooming away in South Florida gardens. If you receive a poinsettia plant as a present or buy them as holiday decorations, you can plant them in the garden afterward, where they will actually continue to grow. In fact, poinsettias are quite easy to propagate from cuttings. Just lay them in the shade to harden off

Holiday color

Here's how to cut poinsettias for lasting arrangements: In the cool of the evening, cut flower stems cleanly, and immediately sear each cut end with a candle flame or cigarette lighter to cauterize it. The sap will crackle, smoke, and flare when the flame hits it.

Once welded shut, the poinsettias can be used in arrangements with or without water, and can usually be counted on to last as long as a week.

for a week or so before you pot them up. Next year you'll be able to give your friends holiday poinsettias from your own garden.Poinsettias are naturals to symbolize the December holidays. Allowed to follow their natural growth and blooming cycle, they produce, year after year, more or less on schedule, huge crimson blooms on long, arching stems. Technically, the showy red leaves are not the flowers, but the bracts surrounding the tiny true flowers at their centers. To encourage bushier growth and more reliable on-time blooming, many gardeners pinch their poinsettias, taking out the growing point on each stem. Some pinch just a couple of times a year; others pinch the tips after every six or eight inches of growth. The more you pinch, the bushier the plant, and the more flowers you'll have—but the flowers will be smaller. To ensure December bloom, experience has shown it's best to stop pinching by September 1 so the bracts will have time to develop. Full sun is best for poinsettias. But their internal bloom clocks run according to the number of hours of darkness they receive, so if yours is planted under a streetlamp it could be thrown off schedule, or not bloom at all.

When they begin to show color, poinsettias should be carefully checked from time to time for the appearance of the tomato hornworm—a well camouflaged and ravenous fellow who may try to have your poinsettias for his holiday dinner. He's large enough to pick off by hand, though, so you won't need to spray. Poinsettias must be kept adequately watered, especially when in bloom. Most other euphorbias are tolerant of dry conditions and excellent for xeriscaping.

Gloriosa lily

As glorious as its name, the gloriosa lily grows from an undistinguished-looking bulb usually purchased in a package hanging on a rack in a garden store. Planted near a fence, the bulb will send up an airy vine with an Art Nouveau attitude, from which will emerge stunning filigree lanterns as large as five inches across. Most are red and gold; more rare is the copper and gold variety. Gloriosa lilies make surprisingly good cut flowers and are splendid in mixed bouquets.

Pandanus

The pandanus (*Pandanus utilis*) is often called corkscrew palm, though it is not a palm, because of the spiraling frondish leaves that grow directly from its main branches. It's also called screw pine, but it's not a pine, either. Pandanus's other attractions are the buttressing skirt of roots that join the trunk about three feet above ground, and the interesting textures left on its branches when the leaves fall. Pandanus leaves, three to four feet long and a couple of inches wide, are used in the tropics for hat and basket weaving. Melon-sized green fruits hang from pandanus branches like Christmas balls. The tree can grow 20 to 30 feet tall.

Water gardens

Some of South Florida's most personable plants are those found in water gardens, and more and more people are immersing themselves in their culture. You could probably find a spot for at least a small pond in an average-sized yard. On larger properties, water gardens can be elaborate affairs of ponds and brooks, or even a moat, complete with stepping stones and bridges. A fountain or waterfall can be a nice addition. If you live on a fresh-water lake with sloping banks, you might be able to turn your shallows into a lovely garden—and attract some of South Florida's aquatic birds and other wildlife as a bonus.

Do-it-yourself water gardeners can go one of two basic ways: up or down. If you want an in-the-ground garden, a recess of different depths dug out of sand or rock can be lined with concrete, special vinyl lining fabric, or a preformed pond liner molded with various ledges for plants with different depth requirements. If digging sounds like too much work, especially in rocky soils, you can build an above-ground pond of concrete blocks. The edges of the pond liner, in or above the ground, can be camouflaged with rock ledges and overhanging plants.

Three types of plants grow in water gardens: semi-aquatic plants (papyrus, ferns, spathiphyllums, canna lilies, and many others) that like to grow in the soft, moist soil at the edges of the pond, aquatic plants (water lilies) rooted in pots at various depths in the water, and floating plants (water lettuce, water hyacinths) that bob freely on the surface, their roots trailing through the water.

Water lilies grow best in organic soils rich in manures and humus, their pots weighted down with a top layer of pebbles or sand. Keeping plants at their proper level for blooming (essential, since a lily will have trouble blooming if its stem stops six inches below the surface) requires platforms of appropriate heights. These can be made from concrete blocks painted to match the inside of the pond. The plants are usually fertilized with special pellets pushed into the soil.

There's more to a water garden than plants, however. Fish are usually kept, to eat plant and insect debris and prevent mosquito breeding; frogs eat bugs; tadpoles eat decaying leaves. This makes for a lovely ecosystem until some pest attacks your plants. Because of all the fauna, you can't readily spray the usual insect controls, and must use nontoxic ways to deal with them.

Also, fish, especially in a small, shallow garden, can be at risk. South Florida's summer heat can cook them, and birds will seize every opportunity to gobble them up. To prevent enough of this to maintain your fish stock, your pond should be sufficiently deep to provide some refuge from the predators and heat. And small ponds should be drainable, so you can easily start over if some catastrophe should occur.

You'll find many attractive books on the subject of water gardening (a few are listed at the back of this one), most of which list sources for plants, supplies, and expert help. If you plan to do some water gardening, it's a good idea—as well as a pleasant task—to do a bit of research before you dive in.

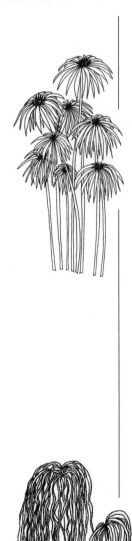

Papyrus

Cyperus papyrus is the biblical swamp plant of ancient Egypt, among whose reeds the infant Moses was said to have been found. Its delicate filigreed seed heads borne on graceful triangular stems can add a classical touch to South Florida gardens. Papyrus grows naturally in boggy places, but will do fine in any sunny area of your garden.

The seedheads of dwarf papyrus, or *Cyperus isocladus*, are shaped like small round balls. This variety loves water, and will grow in pots submerged in a lily pond. *Cyperus alternifolius* is the five-foot-tall umbrella sedge, named for its green umbrella-shaped top. In nature, the umbrella sedge propagates itself by falling over; new plants take root and emerge from the umbrella. If instead you cut off the mature umbrella top and float it in a tub of water, you'll soon have a brand new plant, with roots going straight down through the water, stem sticking straight up. Cyperus are striking in cut arrangements.

Ponytail

Native to Mexico, the ponytail (*Beaucarnea recurvata*), sometimes called the ponytail palm because of its more-or-less palmlike silhouette, is a member of the lily family. It's easily recognized by its bulbous base and the fountain of fine green foliage, like long wavy hair, cascading from its top. Ponytails can be purchased in pots as small as six inches across, but they can grow into multi-branched 20-foot specimens that resemble mystical forests.

Ponytails take years to bloom, but once they do, they usually bloom annually, throwing out big spikes of white flowers. They need little water, making them fine candidates for container gardening and xeriscapes.

Nonstop Vegetables

When it comes to growing vegetables in South Florida, about all those Northern seed-planting charts are good for is mulch. Here in the subtropics, we're hardly concerned about sowing "when all danger of frost is past." We plant in autumn and all winter long, reaping harvest after harvest while Northerners fantasize over their garden catalogs. By the time they start to think about breaking up clods of thawing earth, we're about to sow yet another crop, which we'll harvest just before the summer rains. South Florida gardening die-hards continue to grow some vegetables straight through July and August.

Virtually any vegetable can be grown in South Florida, from spinach and corn to beans and sunflowers. What's fun is to plant what you can grow better, tastier, and less expensively than you can buy at the supermarket— as well as the veggies the supermarkets rarely carry at all. Bell peppers, especially the ones in designer colors, are sometimes so expensive at the store that just being able to snap one off a bush in the backyard is its own reward. Once you've tasted your own fresh garden-grown snow peas, you'll wonder if what they sell in the market shouldn't be called something else. And, sad but true, despite all the hybridizing, chemically treating, and genetic mucking about tried so far, practically the only place a genuine, red, ripe, yummy tomato exists in America today is in backyard vegetable gardens.

Backyard gardens are great places to harvest old-time Florida Cracker foods, like sugar cane, pigeon peas (the national dish of the Bahamas, these once grew wild in the vacant lots of South Florida), okra, collards, cherry tomatoes, and hot bird pepper—whose appearance on the dinner plates of young Harold or his brother would produce such howls of agony that their mother had to resort to tying strings around the peppers so she could divert the little devils to dad's dish.

There are some vegetables it probably makes sense not to grow yourself, though, especially if you're new to vegetable gardening. Corn, for instance. Corn is a huge commercial South Florida crop, and the new strains available at the market are so deliciously sweet, improved in quality, and inexpensive that it seems a waste to devote all the space they need to grow at home. Big sprawly things like melons and pumpkins are probably best left for another year or a larger, more advanced garden. The newest varieties of squash, on the other hand, grow on bushy plants that take lots less room than when jungle gyms had to be constructed to accommodate them.

Harold's fried green tomatoes

For best flavor, pick big tomatoes when they're just beginning to turn pink. Cut both ends off, and cut each tomato into four thick slices.

Lubricate a skillet with your choice of oil, cooking spray, or bacon fat. Fry tomato slices over medium heat, wider sides down. When golden brown on the bottom, flip, then sprinkle with parmesan cheese and a little salt and pepper. Continue cooking for two to five minutes until bottom side is brown. Serve immediately. Harold likes them at Sunday brunch, with eggs, sausage, potatoes, and maybe a fried banana.

Also, while most vegetables do just fine here, there are a few that don't. Leaf lettuces are a better choice than head lettuce, for instance. If in doubt, your county agent can advise you.

Kids—even kids who won't eat their spinach and couldn't care less about rose bushes or palm trees—seem to gravitate to the vegetable garden. If you can reserve a square just for them, all the better. Sugar cane is fun to grow from a cutting (get a fresh one from a neighbor or a cane grower). The stalks grow to six feet and, when ripe, can be peeled and chewed. They're crunchy and sweet, and release a sugary juice.

Children also seem to love growing onions and radishes, probably because they come up fast, and they're fun. And kids of all ages enjoy growing sugar peas, the kind that grow in edible pods. Harold says that's because they're "real easy, real cheap, and *real* good."

There is no doubt that a good deal of work is involved in making a vegetable garden and that it will cost some money initially to set up and properly prepare. Still, the rewards far outweigh the effort, and if you prorate the expenses over the life of the garden and figure in the value of what you produce, the investment doesn't amount to much. Anyway, how do you put a monetary value on the taste of a real tomato?

Step 1: Plan and prep

May is a good time to begin planning your first vegetable garden. First, location: a spot that gets full sun all day, is convenient to a water source, and isn't too far from the kitchen door. Next, size: Harold recommends a rectangle four feet wide by 12 feet long for starters. It's narrow enough to let you reach in from both sides to putter and harvest, and it will produce plenty of veggies. Next year, if you decide on a larger garden, another four-by 12-foot patch can be installed beside it, separated from the original by a stepping-stone path. It's not a good idea to make your first garden too big; the bigger the garden, the more work will be required, and too much can be discouraging. Also, clomping around a too-big vegetable garden compacts the soil and makes your shoes dirty.

If the soil in your yard is just a few inches deep on a bed of limestone or sand, you'll probably opt for a raised bed, since a vegetable garden needs to be turned over to a depth of at least 12 inches, and 18 is better. In South Florida, most vegetable gardeners don't waste time thinking about the pros and cons of raised beds. They just go ahead and do it. A raised bed is made by bordering the garden with low walls made of railroad ties, landscape logs, cement blocks, telephone poles, rock, or other framing that will give you a depth of 15 inches above the ground, and contain the soil and additives you'll be pouring in.

If grass now grows inside the raised framing where your vegetable garden will be, you can burn it out with a nonselective herbicide (Round-up or Kleen-up), carefully following label directions. Once the grass has died, you can dump in a truckload of half and half—which the soil company will understand is not milk and cream, but sand and muck, the fundamental gardening soil of South Florida. This soil is anything but sterile. It's likely to contain nematodes, nut grass, weed seeds, and an entire microcosm of the undesirable insect

The well-contained vegetable

If you haven't the space for a four-by-12-foot vegetable patch, or want to try just a few vegetables the first time out, container growing makes a lot of sense. Containers also enable greater control, admit fewer root and fungus problems, and can be moved around.

Nearly any vegetable that will grow in the ground will grow in pots. A single plant will do quite nicely in a 14-inch container; a larger container could hold a good-looking salad: a tomato staked in the center surrounded by a couple of leaf lettuces, a few scallion sets, and a clump of herbs. A long planter 12 to 16 inches deep could sprout a row of carrots. Just for fun, why not have one clay pot for a big frilly cabbage? Or put your potted cherry tomatoes near a porch support and train them right up the post. Harold did, producing a 12-foot cherry tomato plant that produced handfuls of exquisite and luscious little gems.

Containers dry out faster, though, requiring greater attention to watering. And container-grown vegetables need to be fertilized somewhat more frequently.

Something container growers should know is that the darker the color of the pot, the higher the temperature of the soil within. White pots reflect heat; dark ones heat up a plant's root system. One gardener who called Harold for a garden conference had taken all his white concrete containers and painted them black to match his patio furniture—and cooked his vegetables.

and plant world. Fear not. You have plans for them.

Into the bed of soil should be mixed a generous amount of compost or mulch to add organics and texture. Blend everything well with a pitchfork, and—here's the hard part— let it sit for a month or so.

Step 2: De-bug

In July, more organic material should be added. This can be peat moss, composted manure, compost from a compost pile, or additional mulch. The idea is to produce a rich, friable loam—soil that holds water but drains well. The way to tell if the soil is the right consistency (friable) is to grab a handful and squeeze. It's supposed to just fall apart when you open your hand. If it's too loose and sandy, more organics are needed. If it sticks together, coarse sand.

Now is the time to dispatch the bugs and weeds. Before 1993, soil could be sterilized using chemicals. Since the soil fumigants once available to home gardeners were taken off the market, there's now only one way to get rid of nasties before planting your vegetable patch—solarization. Lay a clear plastic sheet over the garden, edge to edge, anchoring it at the corners. After a few weeks, the heat of the sun will kill bugs in the soil and render the weed seeds impotent.

By September, if you're like most gardeners, you'll be itching to plant something. Just one more thing before you do: Broadcast and mix in some more manure and peat moss. Because the soil is sterile, these additives will provide the bacteria needed for essential microbiotic activity. Also add a very light application of a good quality 6-6-6 granular fertilizer (no more than five pounds per 100 square feet, or, for a four-by-12-foot patch, about two and a half pounds), for a gentle kick of nitrogen. A few days later, you can start planting.

Step 3: Seeds or plants?

It's a lot easier to work with the little starter plants you find at garden stores than to grow vegetables from seeds. It might make more sense, too, since just a few of each kind of plant will supply your family and a good part of the block with all it can use. Also, if you plant a hundred Floridade tomato seeds you might miss out on all the other kinds of tomato starter plants just waiting for you to experiment with, to see which you like best.

Something to lean on

One of the easiest ways to support vegetables is with iron rebar. It can be driven with a small sledge hammer into sand, soil, or rock, and is so slim it won't hurt many roots even if you put it right next to an existing five-foot sunflower. For a no-brainer trellis, you can drive in a couple of lengths of rebar and string twine or wire between them for the plants to climb. When vegetable season is over, the rebar stores away in almost no space.

You can make a real trellis from a four-by-eight-foot lattice panel, laid on its side and supported by re-bar or, if you really want to get fancy, wood fence posts. Two panels, stood vertically side by side, will make a higher trellis, which will turn your climbing vegetables into a privacy screen.

Recycling stockings

Old stockings and cut-off pantyhose legs, strong and springy, make good plant ties for tomatoes and pole beans, and even for staking young trees and attaching staghorn ferns to boards and trees.

To preserve domestic tranquility, Harold has learned, it's best to wait until the stockings are discarded before appropriating them.

Hydro-veggies

Hydroponics, or soil-free growing, is still on the leading edge of vegetable gardening science. Commercially, lettuce is frequently grown in Styrofoam rafts floated on a laboratory-controlled river of nutrient-rich water. The seedlings begin at one end of the river and, a couple of weeks later, emerge as mature lettuces ready to harvest. Never having seen soil, the lettuce leaves stay clean, whole, and attractive.

You can try a version of hydroponics with virtually any vegetable. For each plant you'll need a large container (a metal can or plastic bucket will do) in which drainage holes have been poked or drilled about three inches up from the bottom. This ensures water will always remain in the bottom of the container, but that the plant will never be in standing water. Fill the can with an inactive, soil-less medium. Wood shavings are excellent. The young plant, from whose roots all the soil has been rinsed, goes gently into the medium, and the container is placed in the sun.

Twice a day, pour a mixture of water and fertilizer into the can. Nutri-sol, a good fertilizer for all kinds of gardening, is widely recommended for hydroponics. If you catch the overflow in a big saucer, the same solution can be used four or five times before losing its potency. Vegetables grown in soil-less media take about the same time to develop as those grown in soil, and you'll still have to spray and pinch as needed. But the plant should look clean, beautiful, and good enough to eat.

Starter plants also let you manage your garden more easily. When you begin planting in the fall, a long growing season stretches before you—a good nine months, at least. Many backyard vegetable growers have discovered the wisdom of planting just a couple of plants of each type to begin with. Three weeks later they plant another few. Cycling their planting throughout the season, they can reap a continuous harvest right up until summer.

On the other hand, not everything you want to plant may be available already started. Then, seeds are your only remaining alternative.

Whether you use seeds, plants, or a combination, here are a few planting guidelines you may find useful:

• To give starter plants a boost as you plant, you can water them in with a vegetable starter solution or soluble vegetable garden fertilizer. Osmocote makes one.

• Cucumbers, pole beans, snow peas, and other climbing vegetables need support, and even bush tomatoes and eggplants do better when you stake them. Pole beans grow well and look good on wigwams made from crossed and lashed six-foot poles. Pinch tips when the plants reach the pole-tops, and plants will get bushier, picking easier.

• Trellis plants and taller vegetables like collard greens and pole beans should be planted at the north end of the garden so they won't shade their lower-growing neighbors.

• If you have a choice, it's a good idea to select vegetable varieties that have been bred specifically for South Florida. Tomato varieties, for example, are highly specialized, bred for the regional preferences of different parts of the country and resistance to different diseases. This means that, while it's possible to grow the famous Northern tomatoes like Beefsteak and Big Boy, your life will be easier if you stick to the local varieties. They have names like Homestead, Tropic, Walter's, and Floridade. A new variety, Solar Set, fruits into the hotter weather, and may be worth the trouble of tracking down. Given the dominance of mass-market garden centers in South Florida as elsewhere, it's often hard to find some of these local varieties. Your best bet is to try local mom-and-pop nurseries for starter plants or seeds.

I love loofah

Did you know you can grow your own loofah scrubs in South Florida? Loofah is a handsome vine, with luxuriant green leaves and lots of bright yellow flowers—creating a cheerful camouflage for a fence in full sun.

If you want to, you can eat the immature gourds. Or let them grow large and die on the vine, remove their skins, and use the dried skeletons as shower-mitts. Welcomed gift: home-grown loofah in a basket with a bottle of bath and shower gel.

Part of the entertainment of a vegetable garden is being able to experiment. Have you ever grown kohlrabi, lentils, or cassava? How about malanga, vining chayote, Jerusalem artichoke, or spring onions (put in a few sets, and you'll have fresh scallions in about 50 days). Consider black-eyed peas for New Year's and habañero peppers for hot sauce.

A few herbs make a nice complement to the vegetables in a garden. In fact, many gardeners keep a special section of the garden for them, since herb plants can be quite durable, and some grow to a considerable size. Herbs also make handsome, fragrant potted plants.

Step 4: A little WFS for TLC

Vegetables take about the same kind of attention as any other plant. They need water, fertilizer, and occasional pest control spray.

Water is very important to your vegetables. Vegetable plants are small and tender; the South Florida sun is big and hot. But vegetables do not like overhead sprinkling, which can encourage fungus and rot. A soaker hose, or a bubbler nozzle on the end of your hose, laid successively between the rows as each section is thoroughly soaked, works much better. Because many kinds of fungus are soil-borne, splashing water and soil should be kept to a minimum.

Fertilizer should be applied frequently to established plants—as often as every two or three weeks—but with a very light hand. Harold recommends two pounds of granular fertilizer per 100 square feet, which works out to one pound for a four-by-12-foot garden, every two weeks. Granular fertilizers are available specially formulated for vegetable gardens. Manure, seaweed, and other organic fertilizers are also excellent. If ordinary balanced garden fertilizer is all you have in the shed, go ahead and use it. Liquid fertilizer may be used weekly as a soil drench. Just pour it from a sprinkling can over the whole plant, leaves and all. Some gardeners feel it's best to alternate between granular and liquid, so their vegetables will have a

---

It's the berries

If you long for the fresh raspberries you grew up north, consider the Mysore raspberry, a tropical Indian native species whose appearance is similar to the northern black raspberry, but with lots of wicked thorns. With proper care, each cane bears fruit once, in its second season, and should then be cut to the ground. The current year's new canes will bear the following year.

The clothespin caper

A spring-action clothespin will hold berry vines (or any vines) to their wires or supports, leaving both your hands free to cut and secure their permanent ties. When finished with one vine, just move the clothespin to the next.

How to make a tomato ring

The idea is to produce, in a relatively small space, more tomatoes than you and, unless you have an unusually large family, all your relatives can possibly eat. And it is fun. A four-foot ring that will support four tomato plants requires 12-1/2 feet of road mesh, also called concrete wire, available at home and garden stores. For larger or smaller tomato rings, multiply the desired diameter by pi (3.14). The mesh should be four or five feet tall, with open squares at least four inches wide so you can put your hand through to pick the tomatoes.

Start by removing grass from a circular area about six feet across that gets full sun all day. Shape the road mesh into a four-foot ring, hook its ends together, and center it in the bare area. If you think the ring needs extra support, it can be attached to a few lengths of rebar driven in around the perimeter. Pour in soil to a depth of about four inches.

well-balanced diet. Harold sometimes tosses in Osmocote, too. And if all he has in the shed one week is acid-forming gardenia food, he uses some of that. But no high-nitrogen fertilizer, please, and definitely no Milorganite on edible plants. There's no one right thing to do. But there is a wrong thing: to use no fertilizer at all. As Harold says, "Feed them and reap!"

Spray should be used to nip small problems before they become big ones. A vegetable plant's whole life cycle takes place in the relatively brief time between planting and harvesting. Roots developing underground send nutrients to the leaves, which manufacture the food that will produce the harvest you and your family are so eager for. If insects or

Add a four-inch layer of organics—compost, wood chips, or mulch. On top of this, pour another four inches of soil, followed by another four inches of organics. Sprinkle tomato food on top of this parfait, and water well—or use liquid fertilizer. When you're through, the material inside the ring should be about 16 inches deep, and slightly bowled in the middle.

Plant three or four bush tomato plants (three really is ample for even a large family), in the ground *just outside* the mesh, at equal distances around the ring. As they develop, roots will grow through the mesh and into the compost. The tomatoes can be the same variety or different ones—but be sure they're bush tomatoes rather than the vining ones, because they'll grow tall! Water each plant well.

Once the tomatoes are planted, the ring, *not the plants*, should be fertilized weekly, with a small amount of fertilizer (Nutri-sol is a favorite for tomato rings) sprinkled in the bowled center. As the tomatoes grow, they will send their roots into the ring to absorb the moisture and nourishment. Water the ring only when necessary. Tomato rings tend to stay moist. They eventually shade themselves, too, which further conserves water. To support the growing young plants, gently tie them to the ring with strips of soft cloth. Your tender care will be rewarded with hundreds and hundreds of tomatoes.

fungus take charge of the leaves, the garden is defeated.

Organic gardeners, who don't like to use chemicals, try to solve their pest problems by growing more than they need, so the bugs can have some, too. Less generous organic gardeners, or those with smaller gardens, use garlic water, tobacco tea, and other organic solutions to discourage chomping critters.

Even if you are not strictly opposed to chemical controls, they really should be used only when all else fails. The modern practice of IPM (integrated pest management) saves commercial growers millions of dollars in chemical costs, and can save backyard gardeners money, too.

In any case, chemicals are not always needed for pest control. Many bugs can easily be picked off by hand. Five-inch tomato hornworms are fairly easy to spot. Others can be washed off with a jet of water. Group the kids up into a posse and see who can catch the most snails or grasshoppers. Get out your Sherlock Holmes magnifying glass and investigate those suspicious leaf spots. After that, if you absolutely need to spray, the gentlest, planet-friendliest *contact* chemical you can find is the one to use. And be as specific as you can. If mole crickets, those pesky underground borrowers whose favorite dish seems to be vegetable roots, become a problem, for instance, stir a little mole-cricket bait into the soil. As for when to use *systemic* remedies, timing of which is so critical on edible plants, Harold's rule is: *Never*.

Powder insecticides—called some variation of "vegetable garden dust"—can be used, but liquid sprays are generally more effective. This is because they can be aimed upward at the more absorbent undersides of leaves, where insects like to hide, and where dry dust has a harder time sticking. Mix only the amount of liquid required, and spray only until the leaves are wet.

Even the need for fungus preventatives can be reduced by being scrupulously clean about your gardening. For instance, keep any compost or trash piles well away from the vegetable garden; pick off bad leaves as soon as you see them; keep garden tools clean. If you need a fungicide, gentle ones are available

Millie Songdahl's spirited carrots

Slice eight to 10 freshly picked medium carrots into a microwaveable casserole dish. Add a couple of tablespoons of sugar, the grated peel of one orange, and 1/2 to 2/3 cup of vodka (the alcohol will steam away, leaving just the vodka essence to flavor the carrots).

Mix lightly. Dot top of mixture with pieces of butter or margarine. Microwave on high for ten minutes; stir and wave again until carrots are tender.

Harold says you'll never have leftovers.

just for vegetables, as well as combination fungicide and insecticidal sprays called vegetable garden sprays.

Weeds are not just unattractive in a vegetable garden, they're hygienically undesirable. Sucking insects on weeds can pick up viruses and transfer them to your plants; weeds compete for the water and fertilizer you've so tenderly applied; and weeds can shade young seedlings and crowd them out. In a vegetable garden, weeds are quite definitely plants out of place. Since herbicides would be a bad joke in a vegetable garden, there's only one way to get rid of them: Pull 'em up by hand. Several inches of loose mulch over the whole garden will help reduce this chore, but care should be taken to keep the mulch away from vegetable stems. For more about Integrated Pest Management and combatting garden pests, see "Wild Things: Insects, Fungus, and Weeds," page 117.

Step 5: Let's eat!

If you've cycled your planting, you'll probably find yourself feasting on fresh vegetables all winter and spring, and giving lots away to friends and neighbors. Most South Florida gardeners don't do too much vegetable planting after April, though certain vegetables hold up surprisingly well under the powerful subtropical summer sun, notably cherry tomatoes, sweet potatoes, New Zealand spinach, and leaf mustard. Collards, okra, bell peppers and maybe even eggplants, planted the autumn before, can often be kept going through the summer and for a few of seasons after that. Usually, though, most of the garden is turned over after the last harvest of early summer. Harold broadcasts seeds of heat-tolerant annuals—marigolds or zinnias or, one year, 12-foot sunflowers—to hold the soil over the summer rather than abandon it to the weeds. In September you can sterilize again, add more organics, and start the veggie garden afresh.

The Changing Landscape

I n gardens, things grow. In South Florida, things can grow faster than you may have believed possible. Shrubs burgeon, crowding each other or blocking your view from a window. Grass sneaks relentlessly into planting beds and onto the sidewalk no matter how many times you trim it back. Trees at first petite enough to share the sunlight with flowering shrubs grow according to their own stately pace, spreading their branches—and their shade. Shrubs once neatly shaped and cloaked with leaves all the way to the ground may grow into leggy adolescents.

A garden is a work perpetually in progress. As an ancient Chinese proverb advises, "If you want to be happy forever, plant a garden." Plants and trees you once happily dug holes for and watered and fertilized and mulched reward you by demanding regular trimming and shaping. Overcrowded shrubs, or flowering plants whose clashing colors you have put up with long enough, may need to be moved to another part of the garden—or dug up and given to friends. Or you may want to remove more grass and replace it with a swath of new plants—and you may want to try your hand at making some of those new plants yourself. Here are some techniques to help you manage and improve your growing garden, and have a good time doing it.

A good haircut

Most trees and shrubs need to be pruned from time to time. A few need regular attention to keep them in shape; fortunately, some need hardly any pruning at all.

We prune for specific reasons. A tree that has become too dense with branches can be made lighter and brighter by having its canopy thinned and opened by deft pruning. Shrubs are pruned to keep them bushy and well shaped. Dead, weak, diseased, or broken wood on any plant should be pruned out, not only for the looks of the plant, but for its health. And branches that cross or rub, or are aiming in the wrong direction, should similarly be removed.

Harold recommends pruning with an objective eye. "Don't obsess," he advises. "The idea is to make the plant look better after you're finished than before you began."

Small and medium-sized trees can be pruned by a sufficiently strong, knowledgeable do-it-yourselfer. But for large trees, it's probably wisest to call in a professional. Be aware, though, that professionals in the tree-trimming field follow the same 10-80-10 rules as those in other professions: Ten percent are excellent; eighty percent are adequate-to-mediocre; and ten percent are incompetents or scoundrels. Would-be clients are wise to take a look at work their candidates have done before, to avoid hiring smooth-talking "tree surgeons" who, up to a few months before, were operating on baggage at the airport. When

Tree tips

• Suddenly you notice the little tree you planted a few years back is shading out all the grass beneath it. What to do? Remove the struggling grass from trunk to drip-line, cover the bared earth with a few inches of mulch, and plant a circle of shallow-rooted shade-loving plants like ferns, caladiums, bromeliads, or wedelia in the mulch a few feet out from the trunk. Keep it all moist, and the plants will take hold—and take off.

• A damaged or diseased tree must be removed. Should you automatically fill the depression and plant grass? Not necessarily. Think about mulching the area instead, and creating an artistic planting area you won't have to mow.

• All that's left of the tree is a stump a couple of feet high. Must you go to the expense of having it removed, or the effort of killing it with chemicals? Not if it can be worked into the landscape as a pedestal —for a big planter, for instance—or a base for a birdbath or a driftwood tabletop.

• You're concerned the roots of a tree will jack up the driveway. Is root-pruning necessary? Not if you cut back the top. Many people don't realize that a tree's roots will generally shrink back to remain in proportion with the size of its canopy. This is the biological principle behind the art of bonsai.

you look at a tree-trimmer's work, here's how to tell if the professional you're considering is worth his chain saw.

A tree that has been pruned should be indistinguishable from one that hasn't—except that it's lighter, more defined, more open, and more graceful. It should not look like a big round lollipop. The reason is more than esthetic. Thick round trees are far more apt to be taken out by a strong wind than those with open canopies. Branches should be removed where they join the next larger branch, and not chopped off with long ugly stumps protruding. Bark should be neatly cut, not raggedly torn. The remaining scaffolding of branches should be visually balanced and well proportioned. The tree should look as if it was always meant to be that way.

Properly pruning a tree takes time, and therefore is apt to cost a little more money than a hatchet job. Doing it right is well worth the effort. A well-pruned tree is a happy tree. And looking at it will make you happy, too.

If you decide to do the job yourself, here are a few tips to make the job more professional.

Feed first

Since a tree's leaves provide all its nourishment, pruning, which removes many leaves, puts it on an instant diet. If you have maintained a good nutrition program, it'll be well nourished and prepared for the ordeal. When a tree looks sickly or undernourished, many people think it's a kindness to prune, to "give the tree a new start." But such a tree may not have the energy reserves needed to produce new leaves after pruning. Before you perform major surgery, boost the tree's vitality with regular watering and frequent helpings of good nourishment. Once its canopy of leaves is green and growing, the tree will have a better chance of surviving the pruning process.

Pruning time

Trees and shrubs may be pruned all year-round, but the coldest months are not their favorites. Pruning triggers the sprouting of tender new growth, which could then go down in a cold snap—which, as Harold is fond of saying, is "not a thrill a minute for the plant." The safest pruning period is March through September.

Remember that pruning will eliminate the fruits or flowers that would have appeared on those branches that season. You may wish to prune when fruiting or flowering is finished.

It's best to prune in stages, removing a third or less of the canopy at a time. For trees, taking a third a year for three years is a good way to prune. Shrubs can wait just a few weeks or months between sessions.

Don't be shocked

If any branch of the tree you're about to prune touches an overhead wire, call in a pro. Trees can be excellent electrical conductors. Pruning saws can be, too. You want to live to garden another day.

Stamp out stubs

Even though you often see it done by so-called professional tree trimmers, leaving the stub of a limb or branch on a tree or shrub when you prune is not a good idea. The only thing that will provide food for the stub is new green growth, and if there's not enough reserve energy in the plant's tissues to push out the new growth in time, the stub stands a good chance of dying of starvation while it's waiting. Worse, if it dies, it will probably rot—and the rot can spread right down into the heart of the living tissue.

A properly pruned branch is severed just beyond the collar where it joins the next larger limb. The tree's nutrient-rich fluids are pumped past the cut, the collar scars over, and the tree has a far better chance of healing.

To paint or not to paint

Some professionals advise coating cut branches more than two inches across with pruning paint to seal the openings. Others say painting just hides the damage any entering bugs and fungus may do. Harold himself usually doesn't paint cut ends, but says if you think it makes the tree look neater, go ahead.

Choose your weapon—wisely

Whether you prune with pocket pruners, long-handled loppers, or a pruning saw depends more than anything else on the girth of the branch you wish to remove.

Common sense says that if the branch doesn't fit comfortably in the pruners, it's lopper time, and if it's too fat for the loppers, send in the saw. Forcing a too-big branch into the wrong cutting jaws can tear and damage the plant, and it's not great for your equipment, either.

No matter which tool you choose, be sure it's *sharp!*

Shrub sculpting

Shrubs need pruning, too, for many of the same reasons trees do. Mostly we prune shrubs to make them thick, full, and bushy. But some can be "sculpted"—their interiors lightened to make them more transparent and give them more character. This kind of pruning is called sculpting because it removes what's superfluous to your vision of how the shrub should look, in more or less the way a decoy carver pal of Harold's says he "cuts away the part of the wood that doesn't look like a duck."

Sculpting is an especially handy technique for shrubs that, over the years, tend to become somewhat scraggly from the knees down, like hibiscus, pittosporum, and ligustrum. But they, and other tall shrubs (among them *Carissa grandiflora*; gardenias; old bougainvilleas with massive gnarly trunks; and cattleya guava, which has reddish bark, shining leaves, and fruit that tastes like strawberries), can be sculpted into small, graceful, multiple-trunked trees with leafless legs and full tops.

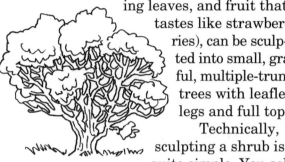

Technically, sculpting a shrub is quite simple. You select the few main trunks and primary branches that will remain, and prune, lop, or saw off everything else to about two thirds up from the ground—or the point at which the canopy becomes green and full. If any new shoots have the audacity to appear on the cleaned trunks, just thumb-prune them.

Artistically, sculpting your first shrub might not be so easy. It may take some time to develop a sense of visual proportion that will enable you to produce a finished shrub that's agreeably balanced. The best sculptors—of stone or shrubs—take the time they need, even if it means interrupting the procedure for a day or so. You'd be surprised how much clearer your vision becomes if you let it rest for a day between sculpting sessions. Sometimes a shrub is so massive, or its branches so tangled and complicated, that you need an assistant to stand back and advise you as you shake various branches. This will help avoid accidentally depriving the shrub of large chunks of its canopy. But try not to be timid about sculpting. If you make a mistake, so what? Call it a revision, an experiment, a change of plan. In any case, the branch will grow back, and you and the shrub will live to resculpt another year.

New plants from old

Advanced gardeners eventually want to do more than plant plants; they want to have a hand in creating new ones. These gardeners are ready to learn how to propagate.

The vegetative part of a plant incorporates everything but the seed-producing flowers or fruit. So vegetative propagation, also

---

Hat-racks are for hats

Under normal circumstances, trees should never be hat-racked (left with only a trunk and the unsightly stumps of a few primary limbs, with little or no foliage). This is because:

• Hat-racking shocks the tree severely, and eliminates its food-producing capability.

• What's left of the exposed branches can be sunburned—often so badly they're trenched right down to the heartwood.

• When the tree is eventually able to produce new growth, it maniacally throws out bunches of shoots from each cut limb, giving you ten times the problem you had before.

• Hat-racking can eventually kill some trees.

• In many South Florida communities, hat-racking is against the law.

Possible exceptions: After a tree has been uprooted, as by a high wind, or when it's about to be moved to a new location, removing the canopy can help it recover more quickly by retaining moisture in its tissues.

called asexual propagation, can be done with any part except the seed. Asexual propagation produces new plants that are virtually exact replicas of their parents, as opposed to sexual reproduction via seeds, which, as we know from human reproductive experience, produces rather less predictable offspring. Most subtropical plants can be asexually propagated by taking a cutting, by dividing a big clump into smaller clumps, by ground layering so a branch will take root, or by air layering—coaxing roots to grow in the middle of a branch, so you can cut the branch off and plant it. Vegetative propagation can also be done by grafting or budding, but these methods require hands-on instruction. If you're interested in learning grafting techniques, good courses are available.

Although propagating can be done (and is, commercially) all year-round, it's much more successful in the warm seasons. Commercial foliage growers heat their propagating benches in winter.

Cut and grow

Some tender branches will grow if you do nothing more than stick them in the ground. Aralia will. So will plumeria, gumbo limbo, arboricola, and poinsettia. But if you start most cuttings in pots you'll have better control over their environment, and therefore perhaps a

---

Rootless wonders

One day, Harold was putting in a plumeria cutting that had been hardening off during the week. His neighbor, recently relocated from Wisconsin, strolled up. "Hey, Harold," the neighbor said. "You aren't going to plant that, are you? It hasn't any roots."

A couple of months later, the neighbor was astounded to see the plumeria cutting had put out a collar of leaves. And a month after that—a flower spike.

Harold next turned a rootless ten-foot limb into a thriving gumbo limbo tree.

The magic works with other shrubs and trees, too, including arelias, dracaenas, ti plants, arboricolas, and lots more.

Experimenting is fun. Harden tender cuttings off by leaving them in the shade for a few days, then stand upright in pots of good soil or in the garden. In most cases, you should keep the soil moist. An exception is plumeria, which should be watered only initially and when it gets dry, or it stands a good chance of rotting.

How to make a mist bed

For a four-by-eight-foot bed—roomy, yet easily reachable from either side—you'll need enough two-by-fours to make a frame for a top of wire road mesh available at builders' supply stores. The framed top can be propped on cement blocks, or you can build legs. You may wish to add a wind baffle on one side of the frame, and something for shade overhead. If the mist bed is sheltered under a tree, these might not be needed. You will definitely need a water supply and electrical current nearby.

Lengthwise down the center of the mesh top goes PVC piping attached to a valved water supply and two electrical time clocks—one set for a 24-hour cycle, the other for a 60-minute cycle—that operate solenoid valves. Mist heads on 12-inch to 18-inch risers, available at PVC sprinkler and irrigation systems supply houses, are inserted into the PVC piping, spaced according to the pattern of their spray.

To operate, turn on the water supply and set the 24-hour clock so the water will be on during daylight hours, off at night. Set the one-hour clock so the mist comes on in short, frequent bursts: a three-second burst every two minutes, a two-second burst every three minutes, or whatever seems best for what you wish to accomplish—which is to keep the leaves of the plant tips you're

better chance of success. Most cuttings should be hardened off by letting them lie in the shade for a few days before putting them into moist soil.

A single 12-foot dracaena, ti plant, or dieffenbachia will produce five or six cuttings of different lengths. Remove all foliage except the very top few leaves of each section, dip their bottoms in Rootone, and stick them all in a community pot of good loose soil, keeping everything moist and shaded. When new shoots appear, dump out the community pot and arrange trios of different heights in smaller pots. Each rooted stem will produce two to four new leafing shoots at the top, and create a lovely decorative plant for use in-

misting constantly moist, but without soaking the rooting material. If the leaves stay moist, science has determined, the tips will root.

Steady the plant tips—a tip is the end of a stem, with a couple of sets of leaves and a growing tip—in their pots, and arrange on the mist bed. A favorite rooting material for use on mist beds is half Perlite (expanded white volcanic material), half peat moss. It's all sterile, so there's little risk of fungus being introduced through the medium. You can use any size containers, from tiny growing trays to six-inch pots for larger plants. In four to six weeks, you can have a whole table full of new, rooted little plants. When you remove the young plants from the mist bed, they should be gently acclimatized (hardened). Let them sit quietly in semi-shade for a while, then pot them up into gallon containers until you're ready to plant them in their permanent locations or give them to friends.

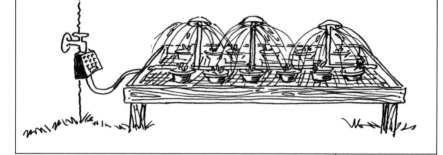

doors or out. The same technique can be used with any cutting, though some, once rooted, prefer to have pots of their own until they are eventually planted in the garden.

Play misty for them

Cuttings you can't get to grow in a simple shaded pot may be a raging success in a mist bed. Misting, or fogging, is how virtually all plants are commercially propagated. The idea is that if you keep the leaves moist but don't let the soil get soggy, a cutting will develop roots.

In a mist bed, you could create enough plants for a whole hedge without purchasing a single one, assuming a friend or neighbor will let you have the cuttings. Misting new plants is done in five stages: 1) start with cuttings from tender plant tips, 2) mist until rooted, 3) move to a shady spot to acclimatize or harden, 4) pot up and move into the sunshine, and, 5) plant in the garden.

Divide and multiply

With some plants, the easiest way to turn one into several is to divide the whole thing—roots and all—into pieces, each of which then develops into a new plant. Ferns, aroids, lilies, liriope, gingers, heliconias, even birds of paradise and orchids can be propagated in this way.

To divide a clump, dig it up, wash the soil from its root mass or rhizomes, and, using a sharp shovel, knife, or pointed pruning shears, cut cleanly between the sections. You can make just a few relatively large plants from the original clump, or divide it into plants of only two or three rhizomes or bibs each. In this way, a two- by two-foot ginger clump can produce as many as 50 new plants.

Except with orchids and bromeliads, it's usually best to shear off all the mature foliage and plant only the short new shoots and the root mass, where the tubers or rhizomes store energy for new growth. Keep the new plants moist and shaded, give them frequent sips of liquid fertilizer, and after a few weeks you should see new sprouts.

Going to ground

Ground layering is the kind of propagation most gardeners discover by chance. When the branch of an agreeable plant rests on the ground — walking iris and shrimp plants do this all the time—the part that touches is often stimulated to throw out a few roots, just for the heck of it. These roots take hold, and, if you cut the newly rooted branch away from its parent, it will grow on its own. Having learned this, you can try it with other plants, too. Brunfelsia, hibiscus, allamanda, and many other shrubs are good candidates. Place soil-filled pots under a plant's branches, then bend the branches down to touch the soil in these pots, anchoring them in position with rocks or U-shaped pins. For good measure, you can score the branch through its cambium layer at the point where it touches the soil in the pot, to make clear to the plant what is expected of it.

Air ways

The idea that root growth is stimulated by the intimate proximity of soil suggests the next logical step: bringing the soil to the branch. This is the principle behind the process of air layering, in which sphagnum moss takes the place of soil (the technique is also called mossing off). Easy plants on which to practice air-layering techniques are hibiscus, key lime trees, most woody vines, crotons, and many flowering trees. Air layering, and in fact all propagation, is best attempted when the weather is warm. Here's how to do it:

• Soak a bunch of sphagnum moss (not peat moss) in a bucket of water. Make sure it gets sopping wet. Have a roll of aluminum foil nearby.

• On the shrub or tree, select a branch about the girth of a finger, and snip off enough twigs and leaves to have a clear space six to eight inches long a couple of feet from the end of the branch.

• Make two crosswise incisions through the bark and cambium layer, about one and a half inches apart, all the way around the branch. For those who really get into air layering, purpose-designed double-bladed pocket knives are available. Remove the bark and soft material between these incisions, being sure not to leave any slivers or bridges of cambium or bark between the two cut edges. Some gardeners like to dab a fingerful of Rootone around the upper edge of the cut end, where the new roots will form. Professional growers are sometimes able to get away with just making a slash through a section of cambium layer and propping the gash open with a small stone or stick, instead of cleaning out a space all the way around. But this method is much less reliable, especially for novices.

• Encase the exposed wood, plus a few inches on each side, with sopping sphagnum from your bucket. Squeeze out all the water to form a moist ball around the bare wood. When you let go, the moss should hold on by itself. This is the medium into which the new roots will grow.

• Wrap the entire ball of moss in aluminum foil, making sure no moss sticks out anywhere. There are two reasons for this:

1) When the moss dries out it will wick moisture away from the rooting area within, and

2) if a bird with homemaking on her mind spies that comfortable-looking sphagnum moss, she may purloin it for her nest! Twist the foil top and bottom making a tight seal through which no air can get in, nor moisture out.

• Go away, and don't come back for six weeks. After that you can carefully undo the foil and have a look. If your layer didn't dry out, you should see new roots emerging from the cut you made. Wrap it up again and wait until the roots start pushing through the foil.

• When you're ready to harvest, clip the branch off *below* the new roots, carefully remove the foil, and place the rooted end of your new plant, still encased in its moss, in a bucket of water. Don't mess with the moss. Treat these air layers gently. If you're too rough, the small new roots will break off. Then you'll have a cutting.

You can plant lots of layers in quick succession by lining them up near the bucket beside a hose and a row of small pots, each half full of good potting soil.

After the roots and clinging moss are thoroughly soaked in the bucket, cut off the old green stem sticking down from beneath the new roots, and steady the root ball, encased in

Plant parenthood

Hybridizing is the process of taking pollen from one plant and carefully placing it on the stigma of another of the same species or genus, in hopes of producing a wonderful new variety. New varieties of orchids, hibiscus, and hybrid tea roses, among others, are created this way.

However, for every cross, scores of different flowers can result; it can take hundreds of tries before there's a single commercial success. Seed farms, which want to avoid cross-pollination, try to make sure both parent plants are the same variety so generation after generation will come true to seed. Many seedlings do not, which is one reason we thin out the scraggly ones.

The costly F-1 hybrid vegetable seeds are produced each and every season from hand-pollinated plants—the only way to be sure the three or four seeds in your expensive packet will grow into the plants you expect.

its moss, on top of the soil in a half-filled pot. Gently add more soil to cover the roots, settling it with a very slow stream of water. Keep the roots still; they're delicate, and packing the earth or twisting the stem can easily break them. Set the pot in a shady spot to acclimatize it; when roots protrude from the bottom of the pot, the new plant is ready for planting in the garden.

Rearranging the garden

In a maturing landscape, transplanting may become a necessary skill. A couple of trees or shrubs originally planted too close together may be squabbling over territory or sunlight. Or you may find, on your travels, a valuable tree destined for the ax, which you could rescue and add to your garden.

Most experts agree the key to successful transplanting is advance planning. This is because the plant to be relocated should have a new set of developing roots before it's moved, and root growing takes some time—six months or more for large or slow-growing trees, six to eight weeks for younger trees, perhaps just a few weeks for shrubs. But this is not always the case. A full-grown elephant ears, for example, can be shoveled out of the ground and relocated immediately. Older leaves will die off, but it's not uncommon to see new ones shooting up within a matter of days. All plants should be well nourished so their leaves can produce lots of energy for robust growth.

For most plants, the best time to transplant is during the rainy season, when earth and air remain relatively moist. The exception, according to most experts, is the live oak, which prefers to be moved during the cooler months.

Ideally, then, at the proper interval prior to the planned move, the well nourished tree or shrub should be root pruned. To root prune, take a sharp shovel and cut a trench around the base of the tree between one and two feet out from the trunk. The larger the tree, the farther out the cut. Use loppers or a saw to cut through large roots. When you're through, the trench surrounding the tree should be a few inches wide and deep enough to see the lowermost roots. However, the anchoring roots beneath the tree should not be pruned. Fill the trench with mulch, wet peat moss, or other organic matter. When a mass of fuzzy new roots appears, you are ready to transplant.

To prepare the tree for the shock of being severed from its spot and relocated, first cut its top back by pruning off at least one third, and as much as half its foliage so the plant won't be able to transpire water from its tissues through its leaves. Next, dig the new hole, preparing it as you would for a new tree, adding manure, filling it with water, and letting it drain.

Now, quickly dig beneath the new roots of the tree, cutting through the remaining old roots to detach the tree completely. Preserve as much of the earth around the root ball as you can. Transport the tree to the new location in a wheelbarrow or with the help of as many pairs of strong arms as needed. If the tree is being moved a long distance, say from your buddy's garden across town, you'll

Plant orientation

It may sound like new-age gardening, but some experts swear a transplanted shrub or tree will do better if you replant it in the same directional orientation it had before.

If you want to see for yourself, mark the north side of the tree or shrub with paint or a ribbon tied to a branch, and replant it with the paint or ribbon facing north. It can't hurt, and it might help.

increase your chances of success by wrapping the root ball in burlap and hand-picking all the remaining leaves. Some nurseries do this as a matter of course.

Gently lower the tree into the hole until the top of the root ball is level with the surrounding earth. Try not to disturb the new roots. Shovel soil into the hole, settling it with water from a slow-running hose. Build a dam of soil around the root basin, and fill the basin with water. Stake the tree to hold it steady, just as you would if it had come balled and burlapped from a nursery.

Of course there is also what Harold calls the "chop-and-hope" method of tree relocation —to be used only in emergencies. One day, long ago, while driving by an oak hammock filled with bulldozers preparing the way for the shopping center known today as Cutler Ridge Mall, Harold spied a small oak tree—maybe 20 feet tall with a four-inch trunk diameter—in the path of destruction. He asked if he could have it, and the dozer operator obligingly ripped it out of the ground and dumped it unceremoniously in a clear area. An inexperienced gardener might have been aghast, and thought the tree had had it, but Harold had known a mango grower who had dynamited his trees out of the ground and successfully transplanted them. He rushed home, dug and prepped a good hole, then snatched up his chain saw and raced back to the tree, where he proceeded to reduce its height to about nine feet.

He clipped the roots clean, shook the rock off, took off additional foliage to diminish the effects of the inevitable shock, and drove home with

his prize tied to his car, its piti-
ful top dragging on the pavement behind him. This poor
little tree was torn out of the
ground. It was given no chance
to develop fuzzy new roots. It
was dumped, dragged, and
man-handled. But in Harold's
hole, full of leaf mold and composted horse manure, the little
tree thought it had gone to
heaven. After a few
weeks of daily watering,
the remaining leaves
were still green.
In time, the oak
sprouted and grew.

Newly trans-
planted shrubs and
trees should be watered
daily for at least a week, every other day for
another week, and as necessary thereafter.
Feed with liquid fertilizer weekly for a month,
then with a handful of balanced fertilizer
monthly for a year. Then put them on your
garden's regular feeding schedule.

Don't be overly concerned about dying,
dropping leaves following transplanting. The
tree is not trying to make you feel guilty
(though you assuredly will), but employing a
radical defense mechanism designed by nature to conserve fluids within the plant's tissues. New growth should appear in two to four
weeks, except in winter, when things can take
longer. If you're not sure whether the plant is
dead or alive, scratch off a little of its tender
bark with a pocket knife or your thumbnail. If
the underlying tissue is green, the plant is alive.
If it appears brown and dry, don't be too hard
on yourself. Even the most seasoned gardener
—even Harold!—loses a patient now and then.

Grass on the move

If you're taking out an area of
lawn in preparation for planting
shrubs, try cutting it with your
shovel into squares or rectangles of manageable size, un-
dercutting to their centers. This
homemade sod can be folded
over and carried or moved via
wheelbarrow to a bare spot you
want to fill. Water daily as if it
were new, purchased sod.

Finding time

Gardeners love to garden. The idea of actually deriving pleasure from working outdoors, even in the heat of summer, even on weekdays before getting ready for work, often mystifies nongardeners—though it's amazing how many nongardeners marry gardeners just the same. Many gardeners will happily rise an hour earlier than the rest of the household to put in some time watering, spraying, pulling weeds, or just strolling around with the hand pruners—always with the hand pruners—observing, gathering intelligence, marveling at the spider webs jeweled with dew, greeting the awakening birds and the already industrious bees, and admiring the amazing beauty of their gardens in the early morning light.

Late afternoon and evening are good times for South Florida gardening, too. As cooks assert that cooking relaxes them, so gardeners relax after a day of work or family responsibilities by mowing the lawn or engrossing themselves in the training of a tree. Weekends, of course, are for the big, grubby, down-and-dirty jobs, like planting, transplanting, major pruning, and hedge clipping . The kind of gardening that works up a sweat and makes a frosty glass of iced tea—flavored with your own key limes, of course—taste like ambrosia.

Within the restrictions of time and temperature, as long as you're somewhat organized, you can stay fairly even. If you go away for a month's vacation, or postpone your hedge trimming too long, there might be some catching up to do, but as long as you don't feel rushed or overwhelmed, chances are you're doing things right. Try to remember to take time to relax. After you've pruned the shrubs or dead-headed the rose bushes, allow yourself the enjoyment of standing back and really appreciating how nice it all looks.

Pace yourself by taking frequent breaks—even, Harold says, if someone inquires sweetly from the doorway, "Are you taking another break?" Relish the sense of accomplishment that comes with gradually making your tiny piece of the planet abundant, fruitful, and a pleasure to behold. And practice accepting with grace your neighbors' accolades, for they will come.

Helpful Information

Your Gardener's Cupboard

very gardener needs some basic equipment with which to practice his or her art and avocation. In the subtropics, some of this equipment may be identical to tools you've used up north. Some may be versions adapted for our soils and plants. Others may be completely new to you. But once you've planned your garden, you'll need them to execute that plan. Here's a list of the fundamental good gardening gear every South Florida gardener should have.

For digging

Digging bar. A heavy metal bar about six feet long, chisel-tipped at one end, for chipping through the recalcitrant limestone rock in which many South Floridians must garden. A pick-ax might be useful (you might wish for a jackhammer, but these are harder to come by).

Shovels. One round-nose, one flat.

Hand trowels. Various widths.

Fork/hatchet. A tool for scraping mulch, digging out roots, miscellaneous jobs.

For watering

Hoses. Long enough to reach your whole yard, with nozzles and sprinkler attachments.

Snap-on hose-end adapters. Make

switching nozzles and sprinklers simple.

Watering can. With detachable head.

For using fertilizer and chemicals

Measuring cups and spoons.

Covered plastic containers. For fertilizers and pesticides.

Empty cans and plastic containers. Various sizes for scooping fertilizers, scattering granular insecticides, and hunting critters.

Hose-end sprayer. For applying large amounts of nutritional and other chemicals.

Pump or battery-powered one-gallon sprayer. For applying moderate amounts of chemicals.

Hand-trigger quart-size spray bottles. For applying small amounts of chemicals.

For lawn and yard care

Lawn mower. Rotary or reel type, depending on your kind of grass. The easiest on you are the mulching mowers that pulverize grass clippings into tiny shreds and recycle them into the grass.

Lawn edger. To keep grass neat along sidewalks, roadways, and planting beds.

String trimmer. For wacking off the weeds.

Rakes. Hard-toothed to level soil, fan-shaped for leaves.

Wheelbarrow or cart. For hauling stuff from where it is to where you need it.

Tool deals

Check garage sales and flea markets for good used garden implements.

Paint your wagon, etc.

If you paint the handles of your garden tools bright colors, you will be able to spot them more quickly among the greenery—and they'll be more easily identifiable if your neighbors are the borrowing kind.

Nail tip

Nails stay cleaner if you scrape them on a bar of soap or rub them in a bit of liquid detergent before putting on your gloves.

For grooming

Pocket pruning sheers.
Long-handled loppers.
Pruning saw.
Chain saw. Plus spare chains, fuel, and lubricant.
File or sharpening stone. To keep all edges sharp.
Staking supplies. Rebar in various lengths, tomato stakes, bamboo canes. Small sledge hammer. Green staking tape, rag strips, old nylons.

For record keeping

Garden plan. To be kept up to date as you develop your garden.
Plant labels. Use with waterproof pens or pencils.
Notebook. For recording names, dates, pictures, important events.

For your health and comfort

Gloves. Leather work gloves, goatskin pruning gloves, and a supply of latex gloves.
Kneeling pad.
Safety equipment. Protective goggles, breathing filters, etc., in case you need them.
Potting bench. Nice to have in a convenient shady spot.

Outside line

A portable telephone will keep you in touch with the outside world (assuming you want to be available). A portable radio can keep you informed and entertained while you garden.

Ray bans

Keep sunscreen, sunglasses, and a broad-brimmed or peaked hat with your gardening tools to protect your skin, head, and eyes from the sun— and use them!

Advice and Education

County Cooperative Extension Services

A government-sponsored office in each county, offering soil sampling, problem solving, and educational services.

Brevard County

3695 Lake Dr.
Cocoa FL 32926
(407) 633-1702

Broward County

3245 College Ave.
Davie FL 33314
(954) 370-3728

Charlotte County

6900 Florida St.
Punta Gorda FL 33950
(941) 639-6255

Collier County

14700 Immokalee Rd.
Naples FL 33964
(941) 353-4244

Dade County

18710 SW 288th St.
Homestead FL 33030
(305) 248-3311

De Soto County

120 North Volusia Ave.
Arcadia FL 33821
(941) 993-4846

Glades County

Doyle Conner Agri. Center
Highway 27 West
Moorehaven FL 33471
(941) 946-0244

Hendry County

225 Pratt Blvd.
LaBelle FL 33934
(941) 675-5261

Highlands County

4509 West George Blvd.
Sebring FL 33872
(941) 386-6540

Hillsborough County

5339 State Rd. 579
Seffner FL 32584
(813) 744-5519

Indian River County

1028 20th Pl. Suite D
Vero Beach FL 32960
(407) 770-5030

Lee County

3406 Palm Beach Blvd.
Fort Myers FL 33916
(941) 338-3232

Manatee County

1303 17th St. West
Palmetto FL 34221
(941) 722-4524

Martin County

2614 SE Dixie Highway
Stuart FL 34996
(407) 288-5654

Monroe County

5100 College Rd.
Key West FL 33040
(305) 292-4501

Palm Beach County

559 N. Military Trail
W. Palm Beach FL 33415
(407) 233-1712

Pinellas County

12175 125th St. North
Largo FL 34644
(813) 582-2100

Sarasota County

2900 Ringling Blvd.
Sarasota FL 34237
(941) 316-1000

St. Lucie County

8400 Picos Rd. Ste 10
Ft. Pierce FL 34945
(407) 462-1660

Master Gardener Programs

Given by horticulturists at most County Extension offices. Call for schedule in each county.

Workshops and classes

Offered at many public gardens. See page 242.

Gardens to Visit

South Florida's horticultural riches are beautifully displayed at many fine botanical gardens in the area. Most are open all year. Some offer guided tours, workshops, and classes, and have museums, gift shops, bookshops, and cafes within the garden grounds. Best to call before you go for opening hours and additional information.

Brevard County

Florida Institute of Technology Botanical Garden
150 University Blvd., Melbourne
(407) 984-2974
A 30-acre garden with Florida's largest palm collection: 2,000 palm trees representing nearly 100 species. Also on garden grounds, Melbourne's first schoolhouse, built in 1896.

Broward County

Flamingo Gardens and Arboretum
3750 Flamingo Rd., Davie
(954) 473-2955
Fifty-five acres of exotic and tropical trees and plants, with an orange grove, an aviary, and many trail walks among huge old trees.

Butterfly World
36500 West Sample Rd., Coconut Creek
(954) 977-4434
Three acres, half screened as re-creation of tropical rain forest, the other half landscaped with plants local butterflies like, as well as a naturalized pond and an English rose garden.

Collier County

Jungle Larry's Zoological Park and Caribbean Gardens
1590 Goodlette Rd., Naples
(941) 262-5409
Fifty-two acres of tropical gardens featuring natural turn-of-the-century landscaping and wild jungle animals.

Dade County

Fairchild Tropical Garden
10901 Old Cutler Rd., Miami
(305) 667-1651
Eighty-three-acre tropical garden, superbly landscaped, with renowned collections of trees and plants from around the world. Rare plants, orchid house, a sunken garden, and a miniature rainforest.

Fruit & Spice Park
24801 SW 187th Ave., Homestead
(305) 247-5727
More than 500 varieties of tropical fruit, spice, and nut trees, herbs, and vegetables. Rare and tropical fruits for tasting.

Vizcaya Museum and Gardens
3251 South Miami Ave., Miami
(305) 579-2708
Ten acres of formal 16th- and 17th-century French and Italian gardens surrounding an Italian Renaissance–style villa built in 1916.

The Kampong
4013 Douglas Rd., Miami
(305) 442-7169
An 8-1/2-acre education and research garden with tropical fruit trees, flowering trees, and edible, medicinal, and ritualistic plants.

Indian River County

McKee Botanical Gardens
US 1, Vero Beach
(407) 234-3288
A natural hammock setting of 18-1/2 acres restored to its original William Lyman Phillips design, plus 80 acres of natural wetlands along the Indian River.

Lee County

Terry Park
3406 Palm Beach Blvd., Fort Myers
(941) 338-3232
Butterfly garden, demonstration vegetable garden, rare fruit garden, grape arbor, and demonstration xeriscape garden.

ECHO (Environmental Concern for Hunger Organization)
17430 Durrance Rd., North Ft. Myers
(941) 543-3246
A working research and demonstration farm with rainforest and desert greenhouses. Varieties of popular vegetables that do well in the tropics are for sale in adjoining nursery.

Edison-Ford Estates
2350 McGregor Blvd., Ft. Myers
(941) 334-3614
Surrounding the winter homes of Thomas A.
Edison and Henry Ford, 14 riverfront acres of
beautiful landscaping designed by Mr. Edison
himself.

Manatee County

Perennial Garden
1303 17th St. West, Palmetto
(941) 722-4524
A demonstration garden of South Florida
flowering perennials on the grounds of
the County Agricultural Extension
Service.

Monroe County

Sonny McCoy Indigenous Park
White St. at Atlantic Blvd., Key West
(305) 292-8157
Oceanside wildlife preserve and a garden of
native plants.

Lignum Vitae State Botanical Site
Lignum Vitae
(305) 664 4815
On the island of Lignum Vitae, across from
Mile Marker 78.5 in the Keys. A historic Keys
residence with landscaped gardens featuring
lignum vitae trees, reachable only by boat.

Palm Beach County

Mounts Botanical Garden
531 North Military Trail, West Palm Beach
(407) 233-1749
An 11-acre educational garden of tropical fruit trees, flowering trees, native plants around a pond, a rose garden, xeriscape, and gardens for testing annuals, perennials, and grasses.

Pan's Garden
386 Hibiscus Ave., Palm Beach
(407) 832-0731
A small preservation-minded educational garden of native plants in natural pond and upland settings, plus a flower garden display.

Morikami Museum and Japanese Gardens
4000 Morikami Park Rd., Delray Beach
(407) 495-0233
A cluster of charming Japanese gardens including a dry garden, bonsai collection, flowering trees, and a manmade waterfall, plus a Japanese country home, on the waterfront grounds of a museum of Japanese culture.

Sarasota County

Marie Selby Botanical Gardens
811 South Palm Ave., Sarasota
(941) 366-5731
The world's only botanical garden specializing in epiphytes, and an international center for research on orchids, bromeliads, and rainforest ecology. Nine acres include a miniature rainforest, water garden, and a museum of botany and the arts.

St. Lucie County

Heathcote Botanical Garden
210 Savannah Rd., Fort Pierce
(407) 464-4672
An intimate garden with palms, bonsai, orchids and bromeliads, rare fruit, subtropical bulbs, and a "subtropical English border."

Plant Societies

South Florida gardeners and plant collectors may join clubs and societies dedicated to sharing, studying, and learning more about many kinds of plants.

Thriving societies, many with national and international affiliations, are dedicated to the study of aroids, bamboo, bromeliads, cactus and succulents, ferns, rare fruit, hibiscus, heliconias, native plants, flowering tress, orchids, palms, roses, ikebana, bonsai, gesneriads, African violets, carniverous plants, and others.

You can get help in locating a chapter near you by calling your County Cooperative Extension Agent or a nearby public garden, or by asking at specialist nurseries.

You can also learn and socialize with like-minded gardeners at one of the many garden clubs in South Florida. To find one in your area, contact:

The Florida Federation of Garden Clubs
1400 South Denning Dr.
Winter Park FL 32789
(407) 647-7016

Recommended Reading

Apart from *The Art of South Florida Gardening*, few, if any, books on gardening give advice specifically applicable to South Florida. However, some contain excellent landscaping ideas, including how-to instructions for paths, patios, decks, and other arden features. And it's easy to find photographs and descriptions of native and exotic plants for South Florida landscapes. Here are a few the authors of *The Art of South Florida Gardening* can recommend.

Besides checking bookstores and libraries for these and other good books on landscaping and gardening, consider garden centers and the botanical gardens in your area. Many have excellent books for sale.

Landscaping in Florida by Mac Perry. Pineapple Press, Inc., Sarasota. Ideas for landscaping, borders, patios, paths, espalier, fences, and vegetable gardens.

A Guide to Landscaping by Maxine Fortune. Great Outdoors Publishing Company, St. Petersburg.

Complete Guide to Florida Gardening by Stan De Freitas. Taylor Publishing Co., Dallas. Solid gardening advice, some applicable to South Florida.

Gardening in the Tropics by R.E. Holttum and Ivan Enoch. Times Editions, Singapore. An encyclopedic volume of plants and trees from tropical areas around the world, presented with beautiful photos.

Enchanted Ground: Gardening with Nature in the Subtropics by Georgia Tasker and the *Miami Herald*. Softcover, Andrews and McMeel, Kansas City. South Florida gardening from an ecological point of view. Excellent plant-selection guide.

The Trees of Florida: A Reference and Field Guide by Gil Nelson. Pineapple Press, Inc., Sarasota. An illustrated listing of native and exotic trees.

The Container Garden by Nigel Colborn. Little, Brown and Company, Boston. Photographic ideas for terraces, balconies, entrances, patios, and vegetables in containers.

Florida Gardening, Month by Month by Nixon Smiley. Softcover. University of Miami Press, Miami. A classic Florida gardening book, first published in 1957, revised in 1986. Not exclusively for South Florida gardening, but there's plenty to learn from this informative book (or any book by Nixon Smiley).

Tropicals by Gordon Courtright. Timber Press, Portland, OR. Color photos and descriptions of plants that grow in the tropics.

Florida, My Eden by Frederic B. Stresau. Softcover. Florida Classics Library, Port Salerno. A compendium of plants for Florida landscaping, many suitable for South Florida.

Florida Landscape Plants by John V. Watkins and Thomas J. Sheehan. Softcover. University Presses of Florida, Gainesville. A good sourcebook for plants, many suitable for South Florida gardens.

The Book of Twelve for South Florida Gardens by Mabel White Dorn and Marjory Stoneman Douglas. The South Florida Publishing Co., South Miami. Published in 1928, reprinted by the South Florida Horticultural Society. Probably the first gardening book for

South Florida, a presentation of a dozen plants favored for South Florida gardens by its authors, who were, at the time, the president of the South Florida Garden Club, and the Gardening Editor of the *Miami Herald*.

Seashore Plants of South Florida and the Caribbean by David W. Nellis. Pineapple Press, Inc., Sarasota. An excellent source book for seaside gardeners.

Growing Native Plants for Landscape Use in Coastal South Florida by Richard W. Workman. Softcover. The Sanibel-Captiva Conservation Foundation, Inc. Photos and drawings of plants for the coastal garden.

Native Trees and Plants for Florida Landscaping by Charles S. Bush and Julia F. Morton. Florida Department of Agriculture and Conservation Services, Gainesville.

Florida Vegetables by Lewis S. Maxwell. Lewis S. Maxwell, publisher, Tampa. From a series of classic Florida gardening books. Other excellent Lewis Maxwell titles include *Florida Plant Selector*; *Florida Fruit*; *Florida's Poisonous Plants - Snakes - Insects*; *Florida Insects*; and the must-have book for every Florida gardener, *Florida Lawns and Gardens*.

Fragrant Flowers of the South by Eve Miranda. Pineapple Press, Inc., Sarasota. A roster of flowering plants and trees, some suitable for South Florida.

A Field Guide to Florida Critters by Bill Zak. Softcover. Taylor Publishing Company, Dallas TX.

National Audubon Society Field Guide to North American Butterflies. Alfred A. Knopf, New York.

There are many books on specific fruits and plant types—bananas, ferns, bromeliads, aroids, bonsai, cactii, and so forth—that grow in South Florida. Among them are hundreds on orchid culture. Rose books, though usually ravishing to look at, are not likely to provide advice specific to South Florida. Here's a sampling:

The Complete Book of Bananas, by W. O. Lessard. Miami.

Mangos: A Guide to Mangos in Florida. Fairchild Tropical Garden, Miami.

Tropical Fruit Cookbook by Maurice de Verteuil. Great Outdoors Publishing Company, St. Petersburg.

Bamboos by Christine Recht and Max F. Wetterwald. Timber Press, Portland, OR.

Begonias/The Complete Reference Guide by Mildred L. Thompson and Edward J. Thompson. Times Books, New York.

Cycads of the World by David L. Jones. Smithsonian Institution Press, Washington.

Heliconia—an Identification Guide by Fred Berry. Softcover. Smithsonian Institution Press, Washington.

Betrock's Guide to Landscape Palms. Betrock Information Systems, Inc., Cooper City.

The Handbook on Plumeria Culture by Richard and Mary Helen Eggenberger. Softcover.

You'll find many good books on water gardening; here are a few:

Water Gardens by Jacqueline Hériteau and Charles B. Thomas. Houghton Mifflin Company, Boston, New York. How to's and descriptions of many plants, giving planting zones.

The Water Gardener by Anthony Archer-Wills. Barron's Educational Series, Inc. How to plan, construct, care for, and repair water gardens. Supply sources.

Water Gardens, Barron's Educational Series, Inc. Softcover. Good how-to illustrations.

Index

Bell peppers 199, 213
Berms 28
Bermuda grass 90
Bio controls 118
Bird of paradise 29, 74, 189, 226
Bird's nest fern 79
Biscayne Aquifer 26, 164
Black eyed peas 208
Black ironwood 177
Black olive 36
Black sapote 43
Black soil 96
Bleeding heart vine 81
Bletia 158
    See also Orchids
Blolly 177
Blue Daze 11, 76, 172
Bonsai 31, 145
Books recommended 249
Boring insects 131
Bottlebrush 41, 177
Bougainvillea
    16, 24, 29, 69, 81, 177
Brain cactus 193
    See also Euphorbias
Brazilian pepper 25, 34, 142
Bridal bouquet 81
Bromeliads
    10, 75, 80, 83, 145, 150
Brunfelsia 189
    See also Yesterday, today,
    and tomorrow
Budding 9, 223
Bufo marinus 134
    See also Toads
Bulbs 83,195
Buttercup 177
Butterflies 82
    Giant Swallowtail 124

C

Cabbage palm 52
Cactus 145, 162
Caladium 78, 83, 147
    See also Aroids

Calcium 115
Cambium layer 60, 104
    See also Plant physiology
Canadian Express 166
Candelabra euphorbia 193
    See also Brain cactus
Canna lily 83
Carambola 43
Cardboard zamia 190
Carissa grandiflora 172, 221
    See also Natal plum
Carolina jasmine 82
Carrots, recipe 212
Cassava 208
Cassia fistula 41
    See also Golden showers
Caterpillars 124, 125, 135
    See also Chewing
    insects; Worms
  Orange Dog 124
Cattleya guava 177, 221
Celosia 84
Century plant 188
Chamaedorea erumpens 52
    See also Bamboo palm
Chamaerops humilis 52
    See also European fan palm
Chayote 208
Chemical storage 127
Cherry tomatoes 200, 213
Chewing insects 120
Chicle 43
    See also Sapodilla
Chinch bugs 129
  testing for 98
Chocolate pudding tree 43
    See also Black sapote
Chorisia speciosa 42
    See also Silk floss tree
Christmas palm 54
Chrysalidocarpus lutescens 52
    See also Areca palm
Chrysanthemum 84
Cigar orchid 159
Citrus 47, 49, 50, 169

J

Jaboticaba 43
Jacaranda 39, 40, 177
Jamaica caper 177
Jamaican tall coconut 54
Jasmine 29
Jatropha integerrima 193
   See also Euphorbias
Jerusalem artichoke 208
Jerusalem thorn tree 42
   See also Parkinsonia
   aculeata

K

Kalanchoe 172
Kentia palm 53, 79
   See also Palms
Key lime pie, recipe 48
Key West 163
Kohlrabi 208

L

Lady bugs 120, 133
   See also Bio controls
Lady palm 53
Lake Okeechobee 163
Lancepod 42
   See also Trinidad lilac tree
Landscaping 19, 21, 28, 83
Lantana 78
Laurel oak 177
Lawns 87
Lawn pests 98, 99, 100
Lentils 208
Lethal yellowing 54
Lettuce 200
Lignum vitae 177
Ligustrum 65, 69, 172, 221
Ligustrum recurvifolia 65
Ligustrum sinense 69
Lilies 83, 226
Lily turf 76
   See also Mondo grass

Lime ice, recipe 48
Limeade, recipe 48
Liriope 73, 77, 142, 226
Live oak 10, 36, 177
Lizards 133
Lonchocarpus violaceous 42
   See also Lancepod; Trinidad
   lilac tree
Loofah 208
Loquat 131
Lysiloma latisiliqua 38

M

Madagascar jasmine 81
Maggots 124
Magnesium 114
Mahogany 38, 177
Malanga 147, 208
Malayan coconut 54
Mandevilla 81
Manganese 114
Mango pie, recipe 45
Mangos 45
Mangroves 34
Manure 110
   See also Fertilizer: organic
Marie Selby Botanical Gardens
   151
Marigolds 84, 213
Marl 58, 102, 181
   See also Soil: acidity and
   alkalinity
Mastic 177
Maypan coconut 54
Mealy bugs 127, 129
Melaleuca 25, 142
Melons 200
Metro-Rail vine 82
   See also Ficus repens
Mexican flame vine 172
Mexican heather 77
Micro-nutrients 61, 113
   See also Nutritional spray
Mildew 128
   See also Fungus

S

Sabal palm 52
Sago 190
   See also Cycads
Salt-tolerant plants 53, 172
Salvia 84
Sapodilla 43
   See also Chicle
Sapwood 104
   See also Heartwood
Sargent cherry palm 53
Satin leaf 38
Saw palmetto 52
Scale 124, 127, 128
   See also Sucking insects
Scavola 172
Screw pine 195
   See also Corkscrew palm;
   Pandanus
Sea grape 172
Sea lavender 172
Seeds
   flower 85
   vegetable 205
Selloum 76, 79, 177
   See also Aroids; *Philoden-
   dron Selloum*
Serenoa repens 52
   See also Saw palmetto
Shade house 24
Shade plants 79
Shellflower 156
Shrimp plant 80
Shrub sculpting 220
Shrubs 65
   flowering 66
   placement 72
   selection 73
Silk floss tree 42, 177
Silver buttonwood 38, 177
Silver palm 53
Slugs 124, 125
   See also Chewing insects
Snails 124, 125, 212

   See also Chewing insects
Snails, Everglades tree 126
Snow peas 199, 207
Soapberry 177
Society garlic 77, 84
Sod 93
   homemade 233
Soil 181
   acidity and alkalinity 108
   half and half 202
Solarization 204
   See also Nontoxic remedies
Sooty mold 127
South Florida Water Manage-
   ment District 164
Spanish bayonet 24, 172
Spanish moss 150
   See also Bromeliads
Spanish stopper 177
Spathiphyllum 78, 80, 147, 185,
   196
   See also Aroids
Sphagnum moss 227
   See also Air layering
Spider lily 73
Spider plant 77, 181
Spinach 199, 213
Spores 152
   See also Ferns; Fungus
Spreader-sticker 114
   See also Surfactant
Sprengeri 77, 142, 172, 181
   See also Asparagus fern
Spring onions 208
Sprinklers 182
Squash 200
St. Augustine grass 88, 92
Staghorn fern 144
   See also Ferns
Standards 66, 157
Starter plants 205
Stephanotis 81
Storm surge 173
   See also Hurricanes
Strelitzia nicolai 189

Other books of related interest from Pineapple Press

*For a complete catalog, write to Pineapple Press,
P.O. Box 3899, Sarasota FL 34230,
or call 1-800-PINEAPL (746-3275)*

Florida's Birds by Herbert W. Kale II, and David S. Maehr. Comprehensive handbook and guide to identification of Florida birds. Includes more than 325 migrant and resident species. Color illustrations by Karl Karalus.

Fragrant Flowers of the South by Eve Miranda. Guide to 80 species of blooming plants that will provide beauty and fragrance to any Southern garden. Illustrated with color photographs and watercolor paintings.

Growing and Using Exotic Foods by Marian Van Atta. Exotic fruits, vegetables, herbs, and wild edibles you can cultivate in your own backyard.

Growing Family Fruit and Nut Trees by Marian Van Atta with Shirley Wagner. Complete instructions for choosing varieties, planting and cultivation, protection from pests and diseases, plus recipes for enjoying the bountiful harvest.

Landscaping in Florida by Mac Perry. Abundant ideas for entryways, patios, driveways, side yards, multipurpose areas, pools, walkways, and more. Includes drawings, photographs, and charts.

Trees of Florida by Gil Nelson. The first comprehensive guide to Florida's amazing variety of tree species, this book serves as a reference and a field guide.

Seashore Plants of South Florida and the Caribbean by David W. Nellis. Dozens of plant species can survive the unique challenges of living at the edge of the sea. This book describes each, including information on appearance, propagation, uses, and history.